THE BODY LANGUAGE OF LIARS

FROM LITTLE WHITE LIES TO PATHOLOGICAL DECEPTION

How to See Through the Fibs, Frauds, and
Falsehoods People Tell You Every Day

LILLIAN GLASS, PHD

Best-selling author of *Toxic People*

CAREER
PRESS
Pompton Plains, N.J.

THE BODY LANGUAGE OF LIARS
EDITED BY KIRSTEN DALLEY
LAYOUT AND DESIGN BY KARA KUMPEL
Cover design by Brad Foltz/Foltz Design
Printed in the U.S.A.

To order this title, please call toll-free 1-800-CAREER-1 (NJ and Canada: 201-848-0310) to order using VISA or MasterCard, or for further information on books from Career Press.

The Career Press, Inc.
220 West Parkway, Unit 12
Pompton Plains, NJ 07444
www.careerpress.com

Library of Congress Cataloging-in-Publication Data
CIP Data Available Upon Request.

To anyone who has ever felt shock, emotional pain, or heartache after discovering that someone whom you trusted with all your heart, lied to you.

May the pages of this book give you all of the information you will ever need to quickly decipher and unveil who is real and who is phony, who is telling you the truth and who is lying to you.

May what you learn in this book provide you with peace of mind, less stress, and more confidence in your life.

ACKNOWLEDGMENTS

I would like to acknowledge my two precious muses—my beautiful, brilliant, and charismatic mom, Rosalee Glass ("Miss Congeniality"), and my precious, cuddly, incredibly smart baby goldendoodle, Annabella Glass, both of whom always make me smile and count my blessings. Thank you for making my writing breaks fun.

And thank you to my dear literary agent, Paula Munier; to Career Press; and to Jennifer White at Splash News and Mary Velasco at Getty Images, for their assistance in the use of the celebrity photos throughout this book.

CONTENTS

Introduction   11

Part I: Encountering the Liar: Who Lies, and Why?

Chapter 1:   What Is a Lie?   19

Chapter 2:   The Price of a Lie   23

Chapter 3:   The Evolution of a Liar:
             Why Animals (Yes, Animals!), Children,
             and Young People Lie   33

Chapter 4:   The Seven Reasons Adults Lie   45

Chapter 5:   Cyber Liars   57

Part II: Human Lie Detection

Chapter 6:   Instincts and Context   73

Chapter 7:   The Body Language of a Liar   77

Chapter 8:   The Facial Language of a Liar   121

Chapter 9:   The Voice of a Liar:
             Pitch, Volume, Tone, and Pacing   155

Chapter 10: Speech Content: It's Not Just Words   169

Chapter 11: Your Lying Eyes:
             Lovers Who Cheat and Deceive   183

Chapter 12: A Profile of the Most Toxic Liar of All—
             The Psychopath/Sociopath   197

Conclusion: The Catharsis of Discovery   205

Index   209

About the Author   219

INTRODUCTION

Being fooled, conned, duped, or just plain lied to can happen to anyone. It doesn't matter how smart, old, rich, or famous you are. Almost everyone at one point in their life, and in one way or another, has been the victim of a liar—someone who has withheld the truth or given them false information. Whether you have been unfortunate enough to have met up with someone who has scammed you in business; swindled you out of money; betrayed you by spreading falsehoods; stolen your lover, husband, or wife; conned you over the Internet, or "catfished" you by purporting to be someone they were not—rest assured that you are not alone. The world is full of these most toxic of people, the liar.

When you find out that someone whom you once trusted, loved, or respected deceived you, a myriad of strong emotions can arise. These emotions range from feeling shocked, hurt, depressed, sad, and/or angry—sometimes all of them at once. You wonder whom you can really trust or whether you can ever trust again. You even tend to question your own judgment. You may even beat yourself up emotionally as you constantly ask yourself why you didn't see the signs of their lies well ahead of time.

But realistically speaking, how could you have seen the signs if you didn't know what signs to look for?

How could you have known that your spouse was cheating on you, that a suitor you met over the internet was a phony, that your housekeeper was stealing from you, or that your babysitter was neglecting (or worse, abusing) your child? How could you have known that your boss was full of it when he said your performance was great, only to fire you the next day? How could you have possibly known that your coworker was badmouthing you behind your back, or that your employee was bilking funds from the petty cash? How could you have been able to tell that your closest friend was being insincere when she told you that marrying your troubled boyfriend was a great idea? What signals did you miss when your son swore he never experimented with drugs, only to find his bong and a stash of pot under his bed later?

How do you know whether you can trust what you read in the media about certain newsmakers? Is that celebrity couple really in love, or is their relationship merely a PR ploy? How can you be sure your political leaders are telling you the truth, or that those on the world stage aren't really lying to you?

Researcher and pioneer in the field of lying Paul Ekman of the University of California San Francisco studied 12,000 people. He discovered that only a little more than 50 percent of them were able to tell if someone was lying. Thus the odds of being able to figure out whether someone is lying to you are not great. However, these odds can increase dramatically when you know how to read certain signals that will alert you to the fact that someone is not telling the truth. My aim in writing this book is to help you increase those odds. I will teach you how to trust your instincts when you have that "gut feeling" that someone is lying to you. More specifically, I will show you what to look for in terms of possible signals of deception in a person's body language, facial language (expressions and movements), voice patterns, and finally, their speech patterns—how they say what they say and even what they write over the Internet.

Introduction

MY BACKGROUND

As a body language analyst, I have been able to report the deception of newsmakers—politicians, sports figures, world leaders, celebrities, and criminals who appear throughout the media. I have done this for years. I have appeared often on various national television shows such as *20/20, Dr. Phil, Entertainment Tonight, ABC News, Good Morning America, CNN, The Today Show, The Insider, HLN, Discovery Channel, MSNBC,* and many other programs too numerous to list here. I was even the body language expert for *Dancing With the Stars* and *Millionaire Matchmaker.*

In addition, I regularly appear in newspapers, magazines, and all over the Internet, where I comment on whether I think newsmakers are lying or telling the truth. I explore whether celebrity couples are telling the truth about their relationship or just presenting it as a public relations opportunity. As well, I examine whether politicians or world leaders are telling us the truth, or merely reciting some not-very-heartfelt rhetoric. I am constantly asked by the media to examine the body language of those involved in high-profile criminal cases, and whether I think suspects are exhibiting signals of deception or telling the truth. Additionally, I report on whether those newsmakers involved in humiliating public scandals are telling us the truth or lying through their teeth.

I have also drawn on my expertise as a body-language analyst in my lectures to law enforcement across the United States and Canada on how to detect deception during interrogations. Perhaps my biggest achievement was the honor of being invited to speak to the FBI, where my lectures included how to recognize the signals of deception.

Most of my work in the area of recognizing deception has been in the legal field, where I have assisted attorneys in picking up relevant information during their questioning of witnesses, as well as focusing the direction of their case. From analyzing surveillance tapes of a drug bust, deposition tapes, interrogation tapes of those involved in child molestation and sexual harassment and abuse cases, to studying the movements of suspects, plaintiffs, defendants, and key witnesses during trial, I have been able to pick out specific instances of possible signs of deception. I decided to share the same techniques I use in my professional life with you throughout the pages of this book. I wanted to do this to empower you to be able to tell who is and who is not telling the truth—simply by looking at their body and facial movements, listening to how they sound, and deciphering what they say.

LYING NEWSMAKERS

The specific signals of deception will be permanently etched into your brain as you see actual photos taken of newsmakers *as they were engaged in acts of deception.* You will read the actual words they said during interviews or testimonies, which also help to illustrate their deception. You will be able to point out specific body language and facial signals, or "tells," that you may have previously overlooked or ignored. Now, it will all begin to make sense when you see the signals occurring at the *exact moment* they lied.

You will now see these photos with a new set of eyes, from a different perspective. For instance, you will notice the nuances of former President Clinton's facial expressions and body movements, and understand more about signals of deception that could be heard in his voice when he pointed his finger and angrily stated, "I did not have sex with that woman—Ms. Lewinsky." You will see signals of deception of other politicians and even understand what signals former Presidential candidate John Edwards gave off when he lied about the paternity of his child with mistress Rielle Hunter during an ABC *Nightline* interview.

You will discover the actual moment various criminals in the news—everyone from O.J. Simpson, Jerry Sandusky, and Scott and Drew Peterson, to financial schemer Bernard Madoff and a host of others—have engaged in deception. You will even learn how to profile the deceptive patterns of the most toxic of liars, the sociopath, by looking at the traits and MO's of such conscienceless criminals as Ted Bundy and Charles Manson. You will also examine the body and facial language of disgraced athletes who lied, such as Lance Armstrong and Barry Bonds, as well as troubled entertainers such as actress and wild child Lindsay Lohan. In looking at photos of celebrity couples, you will learn how to tell whether a relationship is in trouble.

Even though a celebrity couple may have insisted to the press that all was well with their relationship, you will clearly see how their body language and facial expressions can tell a much different story. You will see photos depicting the body language of couples such as reality star Kim Kardashian and basketball player Kris Humphries, actors Tom Cruise and Katie Holmes, Ashton Kutcher and Demi Moore, golfer Tiger Woods and model Elin Nordegren, singer Katy Perry and comedic actor Russell Brand, and how it revealed the signals that they were actually headed for a breakup far before their split was made public. You will even note the body language of singer Chris Brown and his girlfriend, Rihanna, after the couple reunited and claimed they were happy together.

Viewing the precise moment newsmakers exhibited deception, whether through a sweaty upper lip, a squinted eye, a clenched jaw, a cocked head, or a pointed finger, will allow you to easily recognize that particular signal of deception in others with whom you live, play, or do business.

WHAT TO EXPECT IN THIS BOOK

This book is divided into two sections. In the first section, you will learn what happens to you emotionally when people lie to you, and the importance of being vigilant during these challenging times. Next, you will discover when and how lying begins, and how it may even be a significant part of normal human development. You will learn why animals, children, teens, and adults lie, and what kinds of lies they tell. You will come to understand how "little white lies" and even bigger lies can be positive and have beneficial effects. Conversely, you will see how lying can destroy lives, as you learn to recognize habitual liars, "catfishers," Internet schemers, and even sociopaths. And, because you can't see or hear someone over the Internet, you will learn about the red flags to look for in peoples' writing that can alert you to possible deception. This section will uncover what signs to look for as you socialize or conduct business online.

The second section of the book provides you with the profile of a liar. You will learn the importance of context and trusting your own instincts, as well as listening to your own body language signals, all of which can clue you in to possibility that someone may be lying to you. You will learn what clues to look for in a liar's body language, facial expressions, voice, and speech patterns. You will essentially learn how to become a human lie detector as you learn the specific signs of lying that present on the human body—the head, eyes, nose, mouth, lips, jaw, teeth, ears, hair, skin, arms, hands, torso, posture, legs, and, finally, feet. You will also learn how to listen to specific speech and vocal patterns and word choices that may reveal the liar. You will even discover key words and phrases and communication signals that liars often use when they speak or write. You will even learn how to use all of these techniques to recognize the most toxic of liars—the sociopath.

NEVER AGAIN!

Today, you cannot be too careful when it comes to determining who is friend or foe, who is honest or who is a liar. Whether buying a car, entering into a new business venture, getting ahead at your job, finding the right mate, remaining in a marriage (or not!), or making sure your kids are not engaging in illegal activities, you have no choice but to be a vigilant observer. You need to know if newsmakers, including your elected officials, are telling the truth or selling you a bill of goods. And, because so much of your socializing and work now take place online, you are at a huge disadvantage if you don't know the signs of cyber liars.

After reading this book, you will never have to be the one who says, "I never saw it coming," "I was ripped off," "I got conned," or "Someone took advantage of me." Now you will be able to see the visual signals and hear the auditory signs of deception well ahead of time so that you never again fall prey to the liar.

***

Editorial note: In an attempt to achieve gender neutrality and avoid awkward sentence structure, we have alternated feminine and masculine pronouns.

CHAPTER 1

WHAT IS A LIE?

Lying is knowingly giving false information or omitting true information. The ultimate negative outcome of lying is that people's lives can be destroyed and even lost. Countries have been invaded and wars have been started, all because of lies—sometimes even a single lie.

Almost every religious doctrine presents lying in a negative light. The Old Testament is filled with references to lying and cheating. The evils of lying to or about other people are highlighted in the Ninth Commandment: "Thou shall not bear false witness against thy neighbor," while the Seventh Commandment states, "Thou shall not commit adultery," which tells us not to lie to or cheat on our spouse. We also read about lies pertaining to material possessions, such as money or coveted objects. Leviticus 19:11 reads, "Ye shall not steal, neither deal falsely...." The New Testament addresses lying unequivocally in Psalm 63:11, which reads, "The mouth of them that speak lies shall be stopped," and in Psalm 120:2, "Deliver my soul, O LORD, from lying lips, and from a deceitful tongue." Similarly, Proverbs 12:22 states that "lying lips are an abomination to the Lord," and John 8:44–45 pulls no punches by telling us that "lying is the native tongue of the devil." The Talmud declares that "God accepts penitence for every sin in the world, save one, the transgression of the evil tongue." And three times a day, observant Jews conclude prayers of silent devotion with these words: "O Lord, guard my tongue from evil and my lips from speaking guile. And to those who slander me, let me give no heed."

Judeo-Christian beliefs are not the only ones that extol the virtues of truth-telling and warn against the perils of lying. Buddhists talk about the Fourth Precept, which states in part, "I undertake the precept to refrain from incorrect speech, ... abstain from falsehood, [and] practice truthfulness." In the Dhammapada, a collection of sayings of the Buddah, one reads, "There is no evil that cannot be done by the liar, who has transgressed the one law of truthfulness and who is indifferent to the world beyond." Sacred Taoist texts highlight the importance of integrity by warning, "Do not assert with your mouth what your heart denies." Likewise, Sikh scripture in the Adi Granth states, "Dishonesty in business or the uttering of lies causes inner sorrow."

Similarly, we have the 10 Yamas (or laws) of Restraint in the Hindu faith. The second restraint is "truthfulness, to refrain from lying and betraying promises and to speak only that which is true, kind, helpful and necessary." In the Hindu scriptures, one reads, "All things are determined by speech; speech is their root, and from speech they proceed. Therefore he who is dishonest with respect to speech is dishonest in everything." Confucianism addresses lying, too, as Confucius himself said in Analect 2:22: "I do not see what use a man can be put to, whose word cannot be trusted."

Islam also prohibits lying, fraud, hypocrisy, and bearing false testimony. The Prophet Muhammad advised Muslims to be honest and truthful. Two notable verses from the Koran that discuss lying: "And cover not Truth with falsehood, nor conceal the truth when ye know [what it is]" (2:42) and "Woe to each sinful dealer in falsehood" (45:7). Thus, according the Koran, Muslims believe that "truthfulness leads to piety, and piety leads to the Paradise."

While all religions prohibit or at least warn against lying and deception, there are some instances in which lying is accepted. In Judaism and Christianity, for example, lying to someone is sometimes permitted for the sake of peace or for the sake of not offending someone. According to Jewish law, a person may lie under certain exceptional circumstances, for example: to provide feelings of comfort; when honesty might cause oneself or another person harm; for the sake of modesty, in order not to appear arrogant; for the sake of decency, such as not telling the truth about intimate matters; and to protect one's property. Indeed, in the Old Testament there are at least two instances where lying produces favorable results. In Exodus 1:15–21, the Hebrew midwives tell Pharaoh a lie, which saves the lives of many Hebrew babies. Another instance can be found in Joshua 2:5, when Rahab lies to protect the Israelite spies.

In Islam, lying may be permissible a) in battle to save one's life, b) in order to bring reconciliation among various peoples, and c) in order to bring reconciliation between a husband and his wife. The same holds true in Buddhism, but to avoid actually stating a falsehood, Buddhists encourage not answering the question, changing the subject, or lying by omission.

No matter what any religious doctrine states, there are times when humanity comes first. Thus, lying is almost always acceptable in order to save lives. During the Nazi invasion of World War II, even the most religious, including priests, nuns, and other clergy people, lied in order to protect others and save the lives of innocent people, whom they hid in their churches, convents, and homes.

CHAPTER 2

THE PRICE OF A LIE

As we have seen in the previous chapter, certain lies are forgivable. Others are not. In fact, there are intolerable lies and acts of betrayal that are devastating to the human spirit. When you find out that someone has lied to you, how you feel about it depends on who is doing the lying, under what circumstances they have lied, and even the age at which you heard the lie.

Lying to a child about the tooth fairy leaving money under her pillow so that she won't feel so bad losing a tooth; lying to a child that there is a Santa Claus so that he can enjoy the spirit and excitement of Christmas; or telling a child a partial truth about where babies come from, because she is too young to understand—all of these lies are part of modern American culture. It's difficult to imagine a child suffering any lasting negative effects on his/her psyche as a result of having been told any of these lies. But lying to children by omitting crucial information, such as the fact that he or she was adopted, can have grave emotional consequences. Oftentimes, the grown child is unable to forgive his/her parents for being truthful.

Sometimes what you perceive as a "little white lie," like shaving a few years off your age, may be considered a pretty big lie by someone else. To the other person, it may be just as serious as finding out you are still married and living with your husband and three kids, after you said you were single and living alone in a studio apartment. So it all depends on how the other person perceives and interprets the lie. What is not a big deal to some may be a huge deal to others. We all perceive and react to lying differently; it all depends on our definition of lying, the degree and type of lie, how we were raised, our personal philosophy, and how we prioritize what is important to us.

CELEBRITY LIARS

Each day we are bombarded with accounts of celebrities engaging in all kinds of lies, from "little white lies" to not-so-white lies. Some celebrities will swear their relationship is still going strong, even though they were just in their attorney's office earlier in the day, signing divorce papers. Other celebrities lie about the fights they get into. Some even lie about their hardcore exercise and diet routine, when they really got liposuction or gastric bypass surgery, as Star Jones, former panelist on ABC's *The View*, did before the truth was exposed. Some will also claim that they work out a lot to explain their rail-thin physique, only to admit later that they were in fact suffering from an eating disorder.

Others will vehemently deny that they drink or do drugs. Only later will you discover that they have been lying, when candid photos surface of them in rehab centers or, more rarely, after they finally admit they have a drug and/or alcohol problem on a talk show, promoting a book or a film. We don't mind these types of lies, because it's understandable why a celebrity would lie about his or her weight or alcohol or drug use. Most of us understand that the celebrity was likely embarrassed or not yet emotionally ready to deal with the problem or discuss it publicly at the time.

But there are lies that many of us *do* mind, especially the lies of betrayal and cheating on a spouse. When it came out that famed *Twilight* star Kristen Stewart lied to her costar and long-time love, Robert Pattinson, and cheated on him with a producer, she quickly discovered that the wrath of her once-loyal fans could be brutal. Their harshness dissipated when she seemingly reconciled with Pattinson and they were seen canoodling during the premier of their film. Country singer LeAnne Rimes has acknowledged publically that she continues to experience the same negative response from her fans for lying and cheating on her ex-husband with a married man, even though she ended up marrying her affair partner. People take these type of lies personally as they often identify with the repercussions. They may have experienced the devastatingly painful and disruptive effects these type of lies had in their own lives, when someone cheated on them or "stole" their love. When we pay money to see people on the big screen or hear their music, and they betray others over and over again with not-so-white lies, we often take it personally, as well. We may find that we suddenly disrespect them and no longer feel inclined to support them or their projects.

We have seen from various celebrity examples how constant or habitual lying can ruin a person's life. We have seen this kind of lying play out to the extreme with actress Lindsay Lohan. We have heard her mother and manager, Dina Lohan, consistently lie to press that her daughter has never had any problems and instead blame everyone for her daughter's troubles (as opposed to examining her own toxic parenting, as evidenced in her propensity to party with own daughter). We have seen how the once promising actress has repeatedly lied about many things, from being "sober," stealing a necklace, and driving a car that had been involved in an accident, to lying to police during their investigation of that accident. At one point the paparazzi snapped photos of Lindsay shopping in New York, when she was allegedly too sick to fly to Los Angeles for a court date. Her lying antics not only turned off some of her fans, who may have viewed her as a sad curiosity, but also some producers who are in a position to hire her. While some are willing to give her a second chance, her lying has had serious consequences for how she is presently perceived.

BETRAYAL AND CRIMES OF PASSION

There is almost nothing worse than discovering that someone you trust and love has been lying to you. The more deeply you care about the person, the stronger and rawer your emotions. These emotions can range from shock and depression to complete catatonic numbness and even blind rage. Feeling betrayed by a close business partner, spouse, or lover with whom you once shared your innermost thoughts and feelings, and whom you trusted with your life and your heart, has all too often turned otherwise calm, cool, collected, law-abiding citizens into violent criminals and even murderers.

This is what happened to Clara Harris, a 45-year-old married dentist and mother of twin boys. She and her husband, David, an orthodontist, were upstanding members of the Houston community and enjoyed all the material comforts and privileges that wealth conferred. Clara thought that they had a loving, idyllic marriage, too—until the day she saw David cheating on her in a parking lot. This usually rational and level-headed woman, overcome with emotion, didn't think about the consequences of her actions. Unfortunately, these consequences landed her with a 20-year prison sentence for running over her husband repeatedly with her car, which killed him.

In the United States, these crimes of passion are often thought to be committed in a state of "temporary insanity," a defense first used in 1859 by Congressman Daniel Sickles of New York, who killed his wife's lover. While the rage of the betrayed spouse or lover is often deep enough to cause him/her to commit bodily harm, thankfully most people are rational enough to not take the law into their own hands, for fear of legal conse-quences and ruining their own lives. Instead, they choose to fight the liar/betrayer in a court of law. It is there that they can safely (and legally) exact their revenge against the person who treated them so unjustly, and whom they once trusted.

Countless people were (and still are) angry at Ponzi schemer Bernard Madoff for destroying their life savings and leaving many formerly wealthy people destitute. Many said that they even had visions of killing him. Thankfully, for their sake, no one acted out their fantasies of murdering him. Many of his investors knew Madoff personally for many years, and even loved him as a member of their own family. They felt that he really cared about them. In reality, they found out that the only thing he cared about was their money and filling his own financial coffers in order to keep his Ponzi scheme alive. This made the revelation of his lying and cheating them that much more emotionally unbearable.

Just as it is devastating to find out someone cheated, lied, and misrep-resented what they would do with your money, it is equally as devastating to discover that someone whom you once loved and with whom you shared a life, misrepresented himself throughout the marriage. It is crushing to finally discover that he wasn't the person you thought he was. I once knew a couple—we'll call them Tom and Shirley—who were happily married for 35 years. They lived an affluent lifestyle, traveling around the world, wearing designer clothing, regularly attending black tie charity benefits, going to the best restaurants, and giving their kids and grandkids everything they wanted. It wasn't until Tom dropped dead of a heart attack at age 60 that Shirley shockingly discovered that Tom had been living not a double life, but a triple life. He had a gay male lover as well as a 22-year-old girlfriend, who also happened to be the mother of his illegitimate 2-year-old son. Both the male lover and the girlfriend immediately surfaced to claim they were in Tom's will. But neither the lover, the girlfriend, his illegitimate son, his legitimate daughters, his four grandchildren, nor Shirley got anything from Tom's will. Tom had run up so much debt, with his lavish spending and failed businesses, including a strip club and porn site that Shirley knew nothing about, that she had to declare bankruptcy. She lost it all. She lost the house, the cars, her social standing, her "friends," and, sadly her hope and faith. The only tears she shed at Tom's funeral were those of anger and deep sadness for being lied to and betrayed all the years they had spent together.

Such betrayal doesn't only happen in the family setting. There are those people who cheat and lie as a part of their business dealings. You may not know them personally, but they can still wreak havoc on your emotions—for example, think of unscrupulous salespeople who sell you an inferior product, or those who promise you a service that you never receive. There are even charity crooks whose only "charity" is their own bank account. There are countless scammers and swindlers out there who are out to get whatever they can from their unsuspecting victims. And then there are those whom you will never know, who steal your identity and claim that they are you. They end up eviscerating you financially and emotionally, while you are left to clean up the damage they caused to your good reputation, your credit, and what is rightfully yours.

MY STORY

I know from first-hand experience just how emotionally devastating it can be when a liar takes what is yours and claims it as their own. While searching on Amazon.com, I discovered that a motivational speaker from Phoenix, Arizona, had appropriated the same title as the best-selling book I wrote 13 years earlier, *Toxic People*. Upon further digging, I discovered that this same woman had copied, word for word, content from another one of my books, *He Says She Says*. She took lists from that book and put them in her own version of *Toxic People*, thus violating my copyright.

Sitting across from this woman while my intellectual property attorney took her deposition, I was stunned at the blatant lies contained in her testimony. She insisted that she did not copy from my book, *He Says She Says*, when in fact the material and phrasing were identical. As I observed her facial expressions and body language, and listened to her tone of voice and the content of what she said, I divined multiple possible signals of deception—from her defensive tone, the throaty, guttural creaking sound of her voice, and the fact that her sentences trailed off, to the fact that she shuffled her feet and looked away as she answered probing questions (for example, where she got the material).

When she stated that "someone" had sent her the material, but was curiously unable to name that "someone," I was even more convinced that she was nothing more than a complete (and not very good) liar.

I sued her, and we ended up going to trial in United States District Court in Los Angeles. The jury obviously agreed with my assessment that Marsha Petrie Sue was not telling the truth. They felt that she had indeed copied my materials, and they unanimously found in my favor, forever branding her as a copyright infringer. My raw emotions began to heal when I won the case. Sticking up for myself, not accepting lies or allowing anyone to take what was rightfully mine, and, finally, seeing justice served all increased my self-worth. Sadly, many people don't take legal action in such scenarios and instead suffer in silence, with no restitution.

WHEN HEROES LIE

It can also be incredibly painful to discover that someone you greatly admire—someone you consider to be a hero—is a liar. So many people admired Presidential candidate John Edwards. He appeared to have it all. He had a promising future and a beautiful family—a grown daughter and two young children conceived later in life. For close to four decades, he was married to a bright and formidable woman who survived the tragic death of their son as well as her own battle with cancer. Edwards was handsome, wealthy, and well-spoken, with a charming Southern accent; he even looked like someone you could picture becoming President of the United States.

But then he lied. He lied to his cancer-stricken wife, and lied to the world that he was not having an affair with his videographer, Rielle Hunter. He lied that the baby she carried and gave birth to was not his. He even concocted a huge lie to hide that lie, enrolling Andrew Young, his campaign manager, to lie on his behalf by pretending that he, Young, was the baby's father, not Edwards. And of course John Edwards lied to the American public when he claimed that he was honest and forthright, and a good husband to Elizabeth. It turned out that he was none of those things.

More recently, the general public discovered that cyclist Lance Armstrong won the Tour de France seven consecutive times, between 1999 and 2005, only because he had been using performance-enhancing drugs. Naturally this angered people all over the world. His vehement denials and his lawsuits against his accusers were not only what enraged people. His image as a wholesome father of three who had survived testicular cancer, and who created the Livestrong Foundation—a foundation to promote good health and support those affected by cancer—made his lies intolerable. As a result, countless people destroyed their yellow Livestrong bracelets in protest against their hero having lived a lie. In polls taken after Armstrong's televised public admission to Oprah Winfrey, that he used drugs and lied, close to 70 percent said they could never forgive him for his lies.

WHEN LIES CAN RUIN YOUR LIFE

About 25 years ago, a 15-year-old girl named Tawana Brawley claimed that a gang of 10 white men of raped her, put her in a trash bag, covered her in feces, scrawled the terrible words "n- - - -r" and "b- - -h" upside down on her body, and carved "KKK" into her shoe. Al Sharpton and other community leaders championed her cause, while attorneys took on her case for free in order to seek justice against the gang of men who, she claimed, had attacked her. But it all turned out to be a lie. Why did she lie? Because he didn't want to incur her stepfather's wrath for coming home late that night.

Her lie destroyed the reputations and the lives of several innocent men. One man was 28-year veteran police officer Harry Crist Jr., who committed suicide a week after the news broke, over a romantic break-up and failing the New York State Police exam. Some community leaders exploited Crist's suicide and accused him of participating in the rape. Steven Pagones, Crist's friend, defended Crist by offering a solid alibi and insisting there was no way Christ had had anything to do with Brawley's alleged rape. As he tried to clear his besmirched dead friend's name, however, fingers began to point his way. Shockingly, Pagones found himself accused of raping Brawley nearly 36 times.

This far-fetched accusation cost Pagones, who was then the Dutchess County prosecutor, his career. It also cost him his marriage. Tawana's lie not only destroyed the lives of the other 10 men she falsely accused, but they created racial tension across the country. The good news is that Steven Pagones, now a private detective, tracked down this now 40-year-old liar (who goes by the name of Tawana Vacenia Thompson Guitierrez) and sued her for close to a half million dollars for defamation, two and a half decades later. How this plays out still remains to be seen.

Many people lie for the most banal of reasons and end up literally destroying the lives of others. In one case I consulted for, with Oklahoma attorney James Murray, a teenager had accused her teacher and basketball coach, Stacey Brewer, of molesting her. The girl claimed the teacher had exposed himself to her and then shared that information with her school friends, who then jumped on the bandwagon and said that they, too, had been molested by the coach. As a result the coach faced 11 felony counts. After I examined the student's body language and communication patterns in her police interrogation, surveillance, and deposition tapes, I identified several signals of deception. Thanks to the diligent work of his attorney, James Murray, along with my critical observations that uncovered the signals of deception in these girls' allegations, the coach was found not guilty by the Logan County District attorney's office.

Another man who was falsely accused of molestation was Darryl Ginyard of Maryland. His wife falsely accused him of molesting his daughters after their divorce. He was able to prove that he didn't do such a thing, and the courts awarded him full custody along with $825,000. Unfortunately, even though the allegations against him were false, they still cost him his job.

While Darryl Ginyard was lucky in that the authorities and the court believed him, there are those like 33-year-old "Fredrick" who are not so lucky. Fredrick married Robin, who already had three children, ages 3, 5, and 7. Throughout their three-year marriage, Robin falsely accused him of cheating. One day, after she spotted him chatting with a coworker, she told him in a jealous rage, "If I can't have you, then no one will." Fredrick assured her once again that he wasn't cheating and brushed off Robin's remark.

A week later he received a visit from the Department of Child Services (DCS) concerning his allegedly having molested the three children. The DCS found nothing when they interviewed all three children. But Robin was determined to destroy Fredrick's life. For whatever reason, Fredrick got caught up in the system after his stepdaughter Amanda recanted and said that had indeed he molested her. Apparently her mother, who was intent on destroying Fredrick's life, coached Amanda to tell the authorities that she had been molested by Fredrick. They believed her. Even though Amanda's stories were inconsistent and didn't make sense, Fredrick found himself in court having to defend himself against the false allegations.

But his attorneys felt Fredrick had nothing to worry about because they had a smoking gun. Apparently, when the social worker asked Amanda to draw her stepfather's genitals, she drew them showing two testicles. But Fredrick only had one testicle. He and his attorneys were sure he would prevail in the case with this information (in addition to a complete lack of evidence, no witnesses, and a little girl answering "I don't know" or "I don't remember" to every question posed to her during the deposition and on the stand). Shockingly, Fredrick did not prevail. He is now serving a life sentence in a state prison for a crime he did not commit.

Perhaps one day, when Amanda grows up, she will recant and tell the truth, as so many women like her have done, who have falsely accused people of sexually molesting them when they were younger. Although many of these men are released from prison once their accusers recant, the irreparable damage is already done. Years of their lives were taken away. They couldn't enjoy their families, attend loved ones' funerals, or see their children graduate from school or get married.

Every day there are countless men and women who are accused of crimes they didn't commit. These false accusations have not only landed them behind bars, but have also landed them on the registered sex offenders list. Those who don't end up behind bars are still confined to a sort of emotional prison, after having lost their jobs, their life's savings, and their families, all because of someone's malicious lies. These incidents dramatically illustrate the nightmarish effect that lying can have on an innocent person's life. This is why it is essential for us to know *all* the signs of a liar. Lies can cause irreparable damage, whether they are motivated by jealousy, greed, or pure malice.

Sometimes lying may not be such a bad thing. In fact, it may be a significant and even necessary part of our development. The fact is, we lie for different reasons at different stages in our life, as we will learn in the next chapter.

CHAPTER 3

THE EVOLUTION OF A LIAR:
WHY ANIMALS (YES, ANIMALS!), CHILDREN, AND
YOUNG PEOPLE LIE

Believe it or not, animals lie all the time because deception is often essential for their survival. That is why various insects and reptiles, such as chameleons, change color or shape to blend in to their environment and hopefully be passed over by a predator.

When a squid encounters a predator, the squid immediately ejects a cloud of ink between itself and the predator. This cloud of ink happens to be the same color and shape as the squid. If all goes well, the predator becomes confused, and the squid scoots away unharmed. When you see a frightened animal with its fur raised, it too is attempting to save its own life. By puffing out its fur, it is giving the illusion that it is bigger than it is. Many mammals do this to ward off potential predators.

Photo 3-1: A chimpanzee grinning. Photo
credit: Eric Isselee/Shutterstock, Inc.

Chimpanzees, our closet genetic ancestors in the animal world, deceive one another all the time. When they are nervous, they will grin widely. When a rival adult male approaches, however, and they don't want him to know they are nervous or in a weaker position, they will often turn away and use their hands to close their lips. They will literally "wipe the grin off their face" so as to not be attacked. As a result, the other chimpanzee will walk away or go about its business, instead of attacking the erstwhile smiling animal, which would have been perceived as being weaker and more vulnerable. Chimpanzees have also been known to deceive humans. At a zoo in Sweden, a chimpanzee was fooling zoo visitors by appearing docile and munching on the apple she held in her hand. But in reality, the chimpanzee was hiding rocks in her other hand because she wanted to assault any visitors that came close to her enclosure, which she did several times.

Elephants have been shown to exhibit deceptive behavior toward one another, according to animal researcher Maxine Morris. In observing elephants at the Washington Park Zoo, Morris found that those elephants that quickly ate their allotted bundle of hay during feeding time, would often sidle up to the slower eating elephants as they (the fast elephants) swung their trunks aimlessly from side to side, a friendly social gesture. But their real aim was not to get chummy. They would do this until they were close enough to the other elephant to quickly grab some of its uneaten hay for themselves to eat.

Other mammals been shown to lie and deceive humans. Take the highly intelligent dolphin. Trainers at the Institute for Marine Mammals Studies taught dolphins to remove trash from the pools by rewarding them with a fish for every haul of trash they brought in. But one female dolphin decided that she wasn't going to bring up all the trash just for one lousy fish. She wanted a lot more fish for her work. So she engaged in some sneaky deception by hiding the trash under a rock at the bottom of the pool. She then brought up the trash and gave it to the trainer one small piece at time, so that she could get a fish with each tiny trash retrieval, thereby increasing the number of fish she received. In essence, she lied to be better compensated for her work.

There is no better example to prove that animals lie than the decades of research done at the Gorilla Institute, which houses Koko, the famed gorilla who communicates in sign language. When Koko was only three years old she broke a toy. When her trainer confronted her about the toy, Koko used sign language to say that Kate (another one of her trainers) had actually broken the toy. When Koko was five, she broke a kitchen counter by sitting on it. When she was asked about what happened, Koko once again blamed it on Kate. Another time Koko was reprimanded by a trainer for chewing on a crayon. She immediately pretended she wasn't chewing it and instead acted as though she was applying it, like lipstick. When she was pressed about what she had done, Koko finally came clean and told the truth, signing that she has been biting the crayon because she was hungry.

Koko also demonstrated a thorough knowledge of lying when she was playing chase with one of her male trainers and gave him a small bite. When asked what she did, she instantly volunteered in sign language, "Not teeth." She not only lied and denied she had used her teeth or even bit the trainer, but she gave away additional information about which she had not yet been confronted. When humans give added, unasked-for information, it is often a signal of deception. Evidently the same applies to gorillas! When Koko's handler confronted her, saying, "Koko, you lied!" a contrite Koko admitted in sign language that she was "bad" and did indeed bite. According to her trainers, Koko's motivation to lie was to avoid punishment.

My six-month-old goldendoodle puppy, Annabella, does a similar thing to avoid being reprimanded when she knows she did something wrong, like peeing on the carpet or grabbing human food off the table. When I confront her, she will often engage in a playful puppy stance with both her front paws on the ground and her rear up in the air, tail wagging. She will then dance around and try to lick me to divert my attention from what she's done. Instead of showing any signs of shame or contrition, her aim is to ingratiate and distract me in hopes that I will forget the whole thing.

Annabella also lies in order to get something she wants, like going outside. She knows how to ring a set of bells attached to the front door to alert me to take her out to relieve herself. Whenever she rings the bells, I diligently take her out. But there are times she rings the bells to go potty, even though she just went potty moments earlier. She doesn't have to go potty; she just wants to go out again, to play and have fun.

While her lying about whereabouts of my possessions is humorous and endearing, it can also be frustrating. One day I was looking for my reading glasses when I noticed out of the corner of my eye that Annabella was playing with them. As soon as she heard my voice asking her where my glasses were, she immediately hid them with her paws. This was her way of lying to me that she didn't have the glasses, when in fact they were tucked neatly under her little paws. Luckily I was able to document her moments of deception in these photographs.

THE INFANT LIAR

Jane would hurriedly dash into the room whenever she heard her three-month-old infant daughter, Amy, crying. Amy cried to let Jane know something was wrong—that she needed to be changed or fed, was too hot or cold, or that her tummy was upset. But as soon as little Amy turned six months old, Jane began to notice that infant Amy was manipulating her. Jane now observed that Amy's cries were different than they were before. Amy's new cry sounded fake, because it immediately stopped as soon as Jane entered the room. At six months old, Amy had figured out that all she

Photos 3-2, 3-3, 3-4, 3-5: Annabella putting her paws over my glasses and pretending that she doesn't have them. Copyright: Dr. Lillian Glass.

had to do was let out a cry and mommy Jane would come running to give her attention whenever she wanted it.

Until recently, most researchers and psychologists believed that children were incapable of lying until they were around four years of age, because of the complexity of language and the development of the brain. But recent studies have revealed that this is not the case. Researchers such as Dr. Vasudevi Reddy of the University of Portsmouth in the United Kingdom have shown that human infants can display signals of deception as young as six months of age, when they quickly learn that engaging in fake crying (pausing until they hear someone responding to them before letting out another cry) and even pretend laughing get them the attention they want.

Dr. Reddy's studies showed that infants cry and laugh at eight months of age in order to distract a parent's attention, just as my beloved puppy, Annabella, has been doing since she was three months old. Dr. Reddy's research has also shown that infants lie by pretending to be in pain or injured in order to gain attention. Cassie, for example, tried to grab a stuffed animal in her crib and fell over as she reached for it. She had fallen over numerous times when reaching for toys in her crib and never cried. She didn't cry this time either, until she looked up and observed her mother watching her. Immediately, she began to wail as though she were terribly injured. As soon as mommy picked her up, of course, the "crying" immediately stopped. In essence, an infant's motivation to lie is in her attempt to control the world around her and to make sure she gets the attention and comfort she needs.

TODDLER LIARS

As gorilla Koko's researchers observed, the more Koko's vocabulary grew, the more tools Koko had to lie. The same is true for toddlers. As they rapidly increase their receptive and expressive communication skills, toddlers have more tools with which to engage in deceptive behavior. Toddler Kirsty's mother placed a cake on the table. She turned her back for a only a few seconds, to get a knife to cut the cake, only to return to the table and find a chunk of the cake missing. When she looked across the room, she saw Kirsty with frosting smeared all over her face and little hands. She immediately asked Kirsty if she ate the cake, to which Kirsty quickly shook her head and replied, "No," all the while continuing to avert her eyes from her mother's gaze.

Clearly Kirsty was lying, as the evidence was all over her face and hands. Perhaps it was her mother's tone of voice that alerted her to the fact that she was about to be punished. If so, toddlers like Kirsty lie to avoid punishment. When little Kirsty realized her mother didn't believe her response, Kirsty *embellished* her lie and said, "Mickey eat cake." Mickey was the family parakeet, who was locked in his cage at the time of the incident. So Kirsty not only lied about eating the cake, but she lied by blaming it on an innocent bystander, the bird. The example of Kirsty illustrates that toddlers may not only lie to avoid punishment, but may also lie to make themselves look good.

As we have seen with infants, toddlers may also lie in an attempt to gain attention and reassurance. Little Ryan wasn't too steady on his feet. He took a spill trying to get from point A to point B and fell flat on his behind. Initially he didn't cry and was ready to pick himself up until he looked back and saw that his dad was watching. He immediately let out a howl as though he were in excruciating pain. As soon as dad came to the rescue, kissed him and picked him up, Ryan immediately stopped crying and began laughing hysterically. He knew exactly what he was doing! He just wanted a little of dad's love and attention, and when he got it, he was tickled—hence, his joyous and self-satisfied laugh.

Toddlers may also lie to avoid inconvenience. When Nancy asked her 2 1/2-year-old if he wet his diaper, he responded with an emphatic no, when in fact his diaper was soaking wet. He lied because he wanted to keep playing with his trucks and didn't feel like being interrupted by a diaper change. According to Dr. Reddy's studies on lying, as toddlers grow older, they continue to lie more often in order to learn what kinds of lies work in certain situations, and what kinds of lies they can get away with. Toddlerhood is also the time children learn the negative consequences of lying. While they often lie to avoid punishment and negative consequences, they soon learn that their lies often result in the same punishment and negative consequences they were initially and ironically trying to avoid.

PRESCHOOL LIARS

Ages three to five is a confusing age group in that this is when the child's fantasy and reality worlds collide. At this stage of development preschoolers continue to lie in order to make themselves look good. They also engage in a great deal of wishful thinking, all of which often results in deceitful behavior. Children of this age often tell you about imaginary friends and imaginary circumstances/scenarios.

After four-year-old Bobby told his mom that he had put away all his toys, she found that they were still spread all over the floor of his room. In his developing mind, his fantasy of imagining that he had actually picked up his toys may have seemed real to him. While he didn't actually pick up the toys, he may have thought about it before he got sidetracked to go out and play. Similarly, mom Karen overheard her preschool son Randy talking to her neighbor and their son about how Randy went to a local farm and played with Mickey Mouse, who gave him a birthday present of Legos. First of all, Randy had never been to the farm; second, Mickey Mouse, whom Randy saw last summer in Disneyland, resides in Disneyland, not on the farm; and third, Randy's birthday wasn't until three more months. Therefore, he never got Legos for his birthday because it wasn't his birthday yet. So Randy told several lies in one.

If we dissect his lies, however, we will see that Randy collapsed his fantasies and his wishful thinking into reality, in order to make himself look good in the eyes of his neighbors. Randy did see a television commercial for the local farm and obviously wanted to go there. He knew that Mickey Mouse lived in some amusement park, so in his fantasy, he placed Mickey at the farm. He also knew his birthday was coming up in a few months and wanted Legos, so this final bit of wishful thinking helped create the basis for his lie. Parents must be particularly vigilant about being consistent during this crucial stage of development and help set their preschooler straight in terms of what is fantasy and what is reality, so that the child learns that it is not acceptable to lie.

GRADE-SCHOOL LIARS

By the time a child attends school, teachers and peers usually reinforce the idea that lying is bad and that one must always tell the truth. Most teachers are on to "the dog ate my homework" excuse and will not let a child get away with lying. Likewise, if a child's fellow students know he is exaggerating or lying, they will usually not hesitate to call him on it. But because school-aged children's desire to fit in and be socially accepted is so strong, they will often continue to make themselves look good even if it means lying. For instance, they may often lie about how well they did on a test when in reality they may not have done very well. They will also continue to lie out of convenience. For example, a child may lie that she took a bath and brushed her teeth when she really didn't, because she was too busy playing video games and didn't want to be inconvenienced.

The concept of truthfulness can be very confusing to the school-aged child whose parents, teachers, and peers have drummed into him that lying is *verboten*. Thus, because his aim is to please, he will often make every effort to tell the truth. But in his attempts at being truthful he may become *too* truthful, and quickly learn that he cannot always tell the truth or he will hurt someone's feelings. Tommy quickly learned that whenever he lied, it meant that he lost his Internet game privileges. So he made it a point to always try to tell the truth. But his strict adherence to truth telling was met with confusion at school, after he got in trouble for making a female classmate cry by telling her the truth—that he didn't want to hold her hand during dance class because he thought she was ugly, smelled bad, and had sweaty hands.

Tommy's parents had to explain to him that "sometimes you have to lie" and not tell the truth in order not to hurt someone's feelings. They explained that even though his infant cousin may look like a monkey without a tail (as he once relayed to them), he must never say that to his aunt or uncle or their feelings would be hurt. So to add to their confusion, children at this age learn that it is sometimes okay to lie by omission and not always share the truth.

It should also be pointed out that this age of development is crucial for parents in avoiding the creation of habitual or pathological liars. Research has shown that children who are severely punished, or given major punishments for minor infractions, will learn that their fear of punishment outweighs their fear of lying. Therefore, because of the negative physical and emotional conditioning, such children may protect themselves by continuing to lie, to the point where they end up becoming habitual or pathological liars.

TEENAGE LIARS

When teenagers lie it is usually to assert their independence and test boundaries so that they can explore the forbidden such as sexuality, drinking, smoking, or even taking drugs. Sheila told her mother she was going over to Jessica's house to study. She even called home at dinner time to ask permission to have dinner with Jessica and her family and stay into the evening, so that they could both study for their exam. Sheila even put Jessica on the phone to reassure her mother that everything was fine with Jessica's family in terms of Sheila coming for dinner. Sheila's mother was thrilled that her daughter was finally becoming serious about her studies so she readily agreed to her daughter's request. Little did she know that Sheila and Jessica were on a double date and that there would be no studying. Sheila's mother called Jessica's home around 9 p.m. to make sure everything was fine and to ask when she should pick up her daughter. It was a huge surprise when Jessica's mother informed her that Sheila had never been there; in fact, she thought Jessica was at Sheila's house having dinner. Sheila lied because she knew her mother wouldn't agree to her going out on a date during the week, let alone go out with a boy her mother didn't know.

If teens are caught in a lie they will often continue to lie in order to protect themselves or to get the demands of their parents, teachers, and even peers off their back. Even when Joe's mother had found several joints in his drawer when she was looking for a pen in his room, Joe insisted that the joints were not his and that someone else must have put them there. Even when pressed, he continued to maintain his innocence, insisting to his mother that he never smoked marijuana, even though he got high almost every day. As you can see from this example, teens will lie to look good in front of others. Joe would never admit that he had ever tried drugs because he would never want his mother to think he was anything but an ideal son.

Teens will also lie to look good in front of their peers, as they crave social acceptance and want desperately to fit in. That is why teen boys will often lie about their sexual experiences in front of their friends. In contrast, teenage girls will often lie about how popular they are, and will often exaggerate and over-dramatize experiences and even feign illness, in order to gain sympathy or attention from peers and family members. If a teenager finds that he can repeatedly get away with lies, he may incorporate lying as a way of life. While he may know that what he is doing is wrong, he may just do it anyway.

Adolescence is the most crucial time in a teen's life. At this time they should be closely monitored by parents and teachers for lying. Authority figures must set boundaries and consequences for lying, to make it more difficult for teens to lie. If not, they will be more likely to carry this toxic behavior into adulthood.

CHAPTER 4
THE SEVEN REASONS ADULTS LIE

While lies can devastate your emotions and your life, as we learned in Chapter 1, lying can also be a major part of human relationships in that it allows us to function and survive in society and the world. As we have already seen in the previous chapter, relationships between teens and their parents appear to be fertile ground for lying, as teens often play cat and mouse to test the boundaries and see what they can get away with. Relationships between couples can also be magnets for "little" deceptions, from how much someone spent on an outfit or a new set of golf clubs to heartbreaking deceptions of "indiscretions" and adultery. There are also certain occupations that seem to be fertile grounds for liars, from all aspects of the entertainment field; the legal field, where attorneys routinely lie on behalf of their clients; journalism, where reporters misrepresent themselves to gain access to good stories; to law enforcement, whose ranks may omit facts, exaggerate, or outright lie in order to get a confession or to recruit someone to help catch the bad guy.

In his 1882 essay "On the Decay of the Art of Lying," Mark Twain argued that "everybody lies—every day; every hour; awake; asleep; in his dreams; in his joy; in his mourning." Most of us lie without even realizing it. Someone asks you how you are and you automatically reply, "Fine." But the truth, of course, is that you are not "fine" at all. You can barely make your monthly mortgage, you think your husband is having an affair, and your child has special needs that aren't being met. If you told people how you really felt each time someone asked you how you were, you would ruin a passing pleasant interaction and turn it into a depressing and awkward experience for all involved.

How many of us tell someone we will call them or see them later when we never have any intention of doing so? We just say it as a nicety in order to be polite. But instead of being polite, we are actually lying. Similarly we will almost always tell someone we haven't seen in a while that she looks great, when in reality we think she looks awful, with her face all Botoxed and her lips all shot up with collagen to the point we barely recognize her. Probably without realizing it, by mentioning to her that she looks good, we are lying.

Perhaps the best illustration of what can happen when someone is *too* truthful can be seen in the classic 1997 movie *Liar Liar,* in which comedian Jim Carrey stars as a successful, fast-talking workaholic attorney who builds his career as a habitual liar. He constantly promises his young son that he'll be with him, yet he always bails at the last minute, even when it comes time for his son's birthday party. The son makes a magical birthday wish that for one full day his father would not be able to tell a lie. The boy's birthday wish comes true, and from then on, Carrey's character can only tell the truth. Everything he does, including admitting that it was he who passed gas on a crowded elevator, lets everyone know exactly what he's thinking. He even tells a new neighbor the reason everyone likes her is because of her large breasts. He tells one coworker that her hair looks awful, another that he's too fat, and another one that she's a slut. He even tells a woman he sleeps with that he had better lovers in the past.

While the film is hilarious, it would not be funny or prudent in real life to admit to everyone exactly what you think of them. You would constantly be insulting and hurting everyone's feelings, hurting your reputation, and, most likely, damaging your own best interests. If you're like most people, you know that this would be tantamount to social suicide. With that in mind, herein are the seven major reasons adults lie.

1. LYING TO AVOID HURTING OTHERS' FEELINGS

The idea of lying to avoid hurting others' feeling is perfectly and hilariously illustrated in the classic *Seinfeld* episode "Ugly Baby." As characters Jerry, Kramer, and Elaine are huddled over a baby crib looking at a new baby, the mother of the baby suddenly asks the group "So—who do you think she looks like?" The mother expects to hear that the baby looks like either her or her husband, not Lyndon Johnson, as Kramer bluntly blurts out. Jerry tries to dismiss what Kramer says as he politely states, "She doesn't look like Lyndon Johnson," to which Kramer immediately retorts, "Yes, she does."

In another episode, Jerry and Elaine go to the Hamptons to visit a new mother, whose baby, based on Jerry and Elaine's facial expressions upon seeing it, is clearly unattractive. The baby's mother then asks, "Isn't he gorgeous?" Elaine struggles and then lies: "Yes, yes. Gorgeous." Jerry says the same thing and agrees that the baby is gorgeous, when the pained look on his face tells us the baby is anything but gorgeous. It isn't until Jerry and Elaine are alone that Elaine mentions how she couldn't even look at the infant "because it looked like a Pekingese," while Jerry agrees and humorously states, "There was too much chlorine in *that* gene pool." Jerry and Elaine don't share their true feelings about the baby with the mother because they don't want to insult her or destroy their relationship with her. Instead they do it privately amongst themselves.

As adults, most of us live by what we were taught as school children— namely, that it is okay to lie in order to prevent hurt feelings. So when Christmas comes around and we get that ugly knitted sweater or another pair of silly looking socks, we smile and say "Thank you"—even though we hate it. We may even send a note or an email stating how much we liked the gift when in reality, we couldn't wait to regift it. Likewise, most smart boyfriends and husbands have learned the hard way that they can't always be 100-percent honest when their woman asks if she looks fat today, if he likes her dress, or if he thinks her new haircut is cute. Most of us want ap- proval from our mates and want them to be attracted to us at all times, so if they tell us we look fat or they hate our hair or our outfit, it is often taken as an ego-damaging bullet that can wound our self-esteem and confidence.

2. LYING FOR ULTERIOR MOTIVES

People lie not only to avoid hurting other's feelings, but also in order to build up people's feelings so that they will respond more favorably to them. They also may do it because they have some ulterior motive, such as keeping their job, making a sale, or even wooing a potential lover. They wield insincere flattery like a weapon to get what they want, get ahead, or gain an added advantage.

The first rule of sales is to get the prospective client on your side. There appears to be no better way to do that than flattery and showering the person with compliments. For example, Jeff had a new job as sales representative, and was assigned to follow veteran salesman Mike around. After watching Mike in action and how he flattered a female client, Jeff remarked, "Sounds like you were seducing her to go on a date, telling her how hot and beautiful she was. Dude, unless someone's blind, there is no way that woman would be called hot or beautiful, let alone average."

Mike immediately replied, "I don't care if she looks like a moose. Every lady is beautiful to me when she gives me her credit card and I charge up a sale. Every woman wants to hear that she is hot and looks good, even if it is a lie. It makes them feel good and, most of all, it makes *me* feel good because my sales figures go up."

Flattering the boss, even though you don't really like him, in order to keep your job; telling a woman she is sexy and beautiful and that you want to spend your life with her, when all you really want to do is get into her pants; or buttering up your dad so he will loan you the car for the evening—all of these are lies that are told for your own gain.

3. LYING FOR SELF-PRESERVATION

Lying can be a vital part of human relationships, as we saw in the *Seinfeld* episodes. It can also be a vital part of our own self-preservation, as the film *Liar Liar* illustrates. You don't want to tell your boss that he is a disgusting slimy pig if you intend on keeping your job, but Jim Carrey's character does just that. Because he cannot tell a lie, he tells his boss (who is sitting in a boardroom with other board members) what he *really* thinks of him. He blurts out that his boss is a "pedantic, pontificating, pretentious bastard, a belligerent old fart, a worthless steaming pile of cow dung." After a few moments of silence and processing what was just said, his boss bursts out in loud laughter and tells Carrey's character how funny he is and how he "loves a good roast." While the boss thinks it's humorous, Carrey's character is actually being very serious.

In real life, most employers would not take kindly to hearing what you really thought of them. If you are too honest, or even if you let your true emotions—especially anger or frustration—show at work, you may soon find yourself out of a job, as Dave did. Dave decided to go out on a limb and share his honest views with his supervisor. He said he didn't like how he was being treated at work, by working extra hours for little pay; he also said that he didn't feel the department was being run efficiently, and that there was a lot of time and energy being wasted on nonsense. When the supervisor took issue and tried to defend her department and how she was doing her job, Dave displayed his frustration by raising his voice. He was emphatic about his criticisms and strongly suggested that changes be made, as he thought the company would end up bankrupt if such wastefulness continued. Instead of taking Dave's honest suggestions to heart, and perhaps making some changes for the good of the company, his supervisor focused on Dave's anger and raised voice. She shared these concerns with her boss, who ended up firing Dave. In essence, Dave was fired for being too honest with his words and his emotions.

Dave was shocked. All he was doing was being honest and helpful—or so he thought. But this event was a life-changing lesson for him. After a year of unemployment, he was finally able to find work. He vowed that from now on, he would to keep his mouth shut and do his job, whether he liked it or not; he also vowed to keep his honest opinions to himself. He learned that if he wanted to preserve his job and keep food on his table, there was such a thing as being too honest.

Lying can be key to self-preservation and survival in certain communities. Police are very well aware that many lie after witnessing a crime because their life may well depend on it. The witness who "talks" will be viewed as a snitch, which may often have serious consequences. Being a snitch, or being on the side of the law, can often be a death knell. So people will usually lie and deny seeing or hearing anything, in an attempt to preserve their own lives and the lives of their loved ones.

Sometimes people lie to preserve a relationship or a marriage, as Nina did. She didn't like having sex with her husband first thing in the morning. But this was his favorite time of day to get frisky. To her it was an annoyance, as she was barely awake, didn't feel presentable, and didn't have sufficient energy until she had her first cup of coffee. But she obliged anyway because she didn't want to rock the boat or, worse, cause him to stray from the marriage, or find another woman with whom he could enjoy morning sex. So she went along with it and faked it so she could keep her marriage and her lifestyle intact.

The most common lies may be those we tell our "frenemies"—people we pretend to be friendly with whom we don't really like. Perhaps you are in the same social sphere as your frenemy, or perhaps your children play with her children, so you don't want to rock the boat. Instead, you grit your teeth and lie through them as you engage in those necessary (if galling) pleasantries.

4. LYING TO PRESENT A FAVORABLE IMAGE AND AVOID REJECTION

The reason why so many people lie about their weight, their height, their job, and their age online is because they want to present a favorable image to prospective mates. Even though they will inevitably have to tell the truth at some point, they are willing to take the initial risk just for the initial opportunity to connect with someone and not be rejected right off the bat.

Marie was very attractive and looked 10 to 15 years younger than her actual 58 years. She was proud of her true age and put it on one of the dating sites. The result was that she didn't get one response. Then she went on another site and lied. She said she was 45. The response was overwhelming. Lying about her age stopped the initial online rejections. When she finally met her match (whom she actually ended up marrying), she came clean and disclosed her real age when they went on their first date. Although her husband was taken aback at first, he ultimately appreciated her admission early on in their relationship. He even told her he understood why she did it. He shared that had she put down her real age, he would never have selected her.

Many people lie by embellishing their experiences in order to make themselves look like fun and exciting people in the eyes of others. Many do this on social networking sites, such as Facebook, while others lie in person directly to family members, friends, colleagues, and acquaintances. Linda took a cruise with her husband to Europe for what she considered to be their second honeymoon. But the trip turned out to be a disaster. She was sick in bed for most of the trip and only saw the ports through her cabin window and in the photos on the travel brochures strewn across her stateroom bed. On the days she was feeling up to getting out of bed, she and her husband constantly bickered and even questioned whether they should stay married to one another.

When Linda went back to work and told her colleagues about her trip, you would never know that it was the same trip she and her husband went on. She lied by describing the beauty of each city and what she saw. She talked about how great the food was, when in reality she could barely eat. Finally she raved about how the trip brought her and her husband closer together and how they were now planning to go a third honeymoon. But, truth be told, the only third honeymoon her husband will ever go on will be the one he takes while accompanied by the woman he marries after he divorces Linda. Linda knew her colleagues would be looking forward to hearing all about the details of the trip when she returned, and she didn't want to disappoint them. So she put on a show to make herself and her experiences look enviable as possible, as she gave all the juicy details of the trip—all which were lies.

Cyclist Lance Armstrong admitted that he continued to lie about his doping because the "story" of a cancer victim who went on to repeatedly win races and start a charity for other cancer survivors was a storyline that sounded good to the public and the press, and made him look noble and heroic. Likewise, famed Notre Dame college football player Manti Te'o claimed that he continued the lie about his girlfriend dying and being buried on the day he won the football game (as fans came out in Hawaiian leis to support him), because he said he felt that the story "sounded good" to fans. He said in interviews that he felt that he would be too embarrassed to admit the truth and didn't want to disappoint his fans, who obviously appreciated his story. In essence, Manti Te'o wanted the public's approval, so to avoid any embarrassment, he continued the lie.

People often lie or embellish their achievements and omit discussing their failures (or lie about what really happened when they failed) in order to make themselves look good to others, so as to not injure their own ego, their self-perception, and how others perceive them.

5. LYING TO AVOID PUNISHMENT

Just as we have seen with animals and toddlers, a strong motivation to lie in adults has its roots in trying to avoid punishment, whether that punishment comes in the form of disapproval from others, the loss of a job, or a prison term. The court system is filled with people who blatantly lie about their innocence in order to avoid punishment. They don't want to pay a fine or go to jail, so they lie. O.J. Simpson exhibited all the signs of lying about the murder of his wife, Nicole, and her friend Ron Goldman, most likely because he wanted to avoid having to spend the rest of his life in prison (which he ended up having to do anyway for committing an-other crime). Likewise, President Clinton lied about his affair with intern Monica Lewinsky because he wanted to avoid the punishment of possibly losing his marriage, his family, and the American public's support. But his lies almost cost him his presidency through impeachment.

This kind of lie is not the sole provenance of the rich and famous, however. Even though Michelle caught her cheating husband red-handed, with records of telephone calls to his mistress, credit card bills from Victoria's Secret for gifts she never received, and receipts from hotel stays and trips she never went on, her husband refused to admit he was having an affair. He continued to lie in order to avoid the financial and emotional punishment of divorce. Similarly, an armed robber who was caught red-handed (there was even video of him committing the robbery) continued to deny that he did it. He vehemently denied that he was anywhere near the location of the robbery in order to avoid the punishment prison time. Even though most death-row inmates typically have a mountain of evi-dence against them, most of them will go to their grave proclaiming their innocence. This validates the theory that the perceived harshness of the punishment is directly proportional to the tenacity of the lie.

6. LYING TO PROTECT OTHERS

People will go to great lengths to lie in order to protect someone they love or admire. Never was such lying so evident than in the Casey Anthony trial, in which a young woman was accused of killing her daughter. While the court system cleared Casey of all wrongdoing, her mother, Cindy Anthony, a nurse, blatantly lied on the stand by saying that she was the one who had been searching for the word "chloroform" on Casey's computer. She claimed that she had done this because she suspected that her smallest dog might be getting poisoned from eating bamboo leaves in the backyard. She said her search started with "chlorophyll" which then somehow led to "chloroform." Cindy Anthony also claimed that a pop-up with the words "neck breaking" appeared on her screen as she was searching for the word "chloroform."

But these statements turned out to be lies. Her nursing supervisor verified that she was at work the day she claimed to be at home on her computer. In addition, a computer forensics expert from Florida's Orange County Sheriff's office also confirmed that there had been no pop-up with the term "neck breaking," but instead that somebody had actively searched for those words. Cindy Anthony's overt lies were almost certainly motivated by her desire to spare her daughter from death row. In essence, she lied to save her daughter's life.

Another example of someone who was willing to lie at all costs in order to save someone's reputation and career was Andrew Aldridge Young, a former campaign worker and assistant to former Presidential candidate John Edwards. Young, who was happily married with three children at the time, publicly claimed to be the father of Rielle Hunter's baby, when in fact it was Edwards' child. He so admired and respected Edwards that he was willing to risk his own reputation and destroy his own life in order to protect Edwards' reputation and his bid for the Presidency.

By way of contrast, lying in order to protect someone's life can be a noble and selfless act, especially when you don't know the person whose life you are saving. There are countless stories of the risks complete strangers took in Eastern Europe during the 1940s in order to save Jews by hiding them. These people were righteous heroes who risked their own lives by lying to the Nazis, with the intention of saving innocent people.

A similarly inspiring story took place three decades after the Holocaust. A Canadian housewife and music professor by the name of Judy Feld Carr saved thousands of Syrian Jews from torture and death through her lies. Using a secret identity, she bribed officials and lied to authorities as, one by one, she smuggled and bought the freedom of about 3,000 people who, thanks to her bravery, have since gone on to raise families and create a new generation as they live free and productive lives.

7. LYING TO MOTIVATE OTHERS

In the 1960s the popular cartoon character Popeye told children that they could grow big and strong like him if they just ate their spinach. In an attempt to get their children to eat their vegetables, parents of that era followed suit by telling their children that they would grow bigger, faster if they ate their vegetables. This lie probably motivated many children to eat a healthier diet. Similarly, many doctors lie to patients to encourage them to not give up hope. They may tell a patient that he will walk again, even though his legs have been shattered in an accident. They will lie in order to get the patient to cooperate, to not give up hope and try his best. Many times these positive, motivating lies become positive, self-fulfilling prophecies for the patient. The patient may indeed be able to walk again or at least improve his condition.

I have done this myself when I worked in the field of speech pathology early on in my career. I once had a very prominent celebrity client who had suffered a stroke. The stroke severely impeded his ability to speak intelligibly. He was overcome by severe depression and even lost the will to live. Although I was aware of the extent of his brain damage, I told him a "little white lie"—a lie that ended up being the catalyst for him to wake up every morning and live to fight through another day. I told him that I was sure he would be on screen again, even though I was not certain that would be the case. I assured him that he had to work hard on his speech and voice exercises and drills, because the public desperately wanted him back. As it turned out he dedicated every waking moment to improving his ability to speak. His progress was remarkable. In a short period of time, this great screen legend actually ended up making a film, in a performance that was well received. In addition, he regularly appeared on television interviews and made countless heartfelt and inspiring acceptance speeches for the numerous awards he received. My "little white lie" had given him hope that there was something ahead that he could look forward to. It gave him that inner fire to never give up, which then allowed him to improve dramatically, relearn how to speak, and then motivate and emotionally touch others in turn.

CHAPTER 5

CYBER LIARS

I f you want to meet someone online or do business with anyone over the Internet, you must exercise vigilance at all times. Research has shown that it is a given that most people lie online. They do this in order to put their best foot forward and attract others. They want your attention to satisfy their intentions as soon as possible.

In terms of online dating, one study showed that 80 percent of people will lie about one or more of their physical attributes, such as age, height, and weight. Women tend to lie more often about their age and their weight, while men tend to lie about their height, their job, their status, and their finances. Another study found that about 30 percent of people are not honest with the photographs they post. With the popularity of online dating services and social networking growing every day, it is essential to know exactly with whom you are communicating—who is real and who is fake. Because you don't have the advantage of having visual and auditory cues at your disposal, you have to rely on the exact words and phrases you read.

People don't just scam you online to build up their own ego in the romantic arena. The Internet is filled with people who will happily take your money and empty your bank account, if you let them. Sometimes people do this stuff just to amuse themselves. Here are some tips to help you weed out online liars and scammers so that you can hit the delete button or block them forever.

1. IT SOUNDS TOO GOOD TO BE TRUE

If someone offers you a business deal that sounds too good to be true, like making money while you sleep or making a year's salary in just a few months, know that he is most likely scamming you. If someone tells you that you don't need any credentials or experience, that's a huge red flag, too.

Immediately hit the delete button if anyone sends you an email about a long lost relative leaving you millions of dollars, but all she needs is your banking information to deposit the money into your account. Likewise, if anyone emails you that he is stuck in a foreign country without money or identification, and only *you* can help him by wiring money, don't do it. He may give you a myriad of reasons as to why he is contacting you, of all people, to help him, but don't fall for it. This is one of the reasons there are embassies in foreign countries, so they can help people out in moments like these. You may think you are being a Good Samaritan if you help someone in need, but if you do, you will soon discover that you have been scammed. Even though it sounds ridiculous, you would be surprised at the countless number of people all across the globe who have fallen for these kinds of scams, only to have their bank accounts emptied.

2. THEY PROFESS THEIR LOVE FOR YOU TOO QUICKLY

If you meet someone on an online dating site and he quickly professes his love to you or tells you he wants you to be the mother of his children—*run.* He wants something from you, but it sure isn't love! This kind of scammer may also try to entice you by saying he wants to see you but can't, because he needs to raise some money. What he is really saying is he wants you to pay for his plane ticket. If you cough up the money, rest assured that it will be the last time you will see your money—or hear from Romeo. He will take your money and run.

If you have just met someone online, and she tells you that she wants to take you away to the Bahamas or some other exotic destination, or she tells you about future plans that involve the two of you, this is a huge red flag that you should run far and fast. Someone like this is very needy, and likely idealizing her fantasy about having a relationship and a future with someone—anyone. You just happen to be the warm body on the other end of the high-speed connection. Putting out these kinds of "carrots" is a ploy to see if you will bite and jump headlong into this desperately manufactured relationship. Unfortunately, people like this usually disappear or bail on the relationship pretty quickly; or, they will still stick around only to suck more money or perks out of you. For you, it might be romance and a future; for her, it is merely a game and all about now.

3. SOB STORIES AND TRAGIC WOES OF PERPETUAL VICTIMS

Anyone you meet online who tells you a tragic or pathetic sob story, who goes on about his woes and how he needs money immediately to pay for his son's life-saving operation, is most likely trying to scam you. If he shares all manner of woes with you after barely knowing you, he is hoping against hope that you will be swayed by his plight and be the one to "help" him. Instead, drop him like a hot potato and hit the delete button. Additionally, if you read an online dating profile that contains a string of tragic woes (she was orphaned, her father left when she was six, her spouse left her or died), she is likely trolling for an overly sympathetic, "bleeding heart" type of person whom she can take advantage of. She is looking for someone to grab onto and help save her. If you are naïve enough to lend her a helping hand, rest assured that she will be pulling on that hand until you are right down there with her. She is looking for an easy victim, someone whom she can manipulate simply by telling her troubles.

Another red flag is someone who tells you how everyone wrongs him. He seems to live life as a perpetual victim; everyone else is to blame for his life circumstances. If you get paranoid vibes from someone like this, listen to your instincts and beware.

4. MULTIPLE INCONSISTENCIES

As get to know someone online, pay attention to the consistency of his statements. If he tells you one thing initially, and then tells you something even marginally different later on, know that he is likely lying to you. Sociopaths will often reveal themselves in this way, as their thought processes are often inconsistent and scattered. So, if someone tells you that he doesn't have kids and then three weeks later tells you he is taking his son to a soccer game, it's a very bad sign. If you confront him and he a.) hems and haws, b.) composes an overly detailed, effusive answer that doesn't gel with what he has revealed initially, or c.) (and this is a big one) gets defensive, know that he most likely has something to hide. If you ask this kind of person a question, and then ask it again but slightly rephrased, you will often hear a different answer. This is a giant, waving red flag that you should stay away from this person. Forewarned is forearmed.

5. SARCASM, NASTINESS, AND THE MACABRE

Someone who starts a cyber relationship by coming across on the offensive—making hostile or attacking comments, or belittling you if you disagree with her or are ignorant about a topic, is probably insecure and at the very least insensitive, and may even be emotionally disturbed. Someone like this may criticize your profile or your photo in a hostile tone. Know that she has a chip on her shoulder and it's not you! She's trying to tap into your insecurities by cutting you down. For instance she may say you have a pretty face but would be prettier if you took off a few pounds. If you react in a dejected manner or make excuses for how you look, instead of saying that you are satisfied with your weight, she now knows your weak spot which she can use to manipulate you.

Many times cyber scammers like this will use their belligerence as a ploy to "test" the person whom they are dealing with. They are letting you know that they are in charge. Know that if you accept rude or mean behavior from a stranger, you are setting yourself up for an abusive interaction and relationship. There are many bona fide sadists out there in cyberspace who are looking for masochists and doormats who will accept their abuse. This is their screening process, so beware.

You should also take references to the macabre, the occult, and the dark side very seriously. If someone threatens you, no matter how thinly veiled the threat, and even if it is followed by LOL, take heed and hit delete. One woman I know agreed to meet a man she met online who had shared with her a Valentine's Day poem he wrote. The poem actually sounded more like a Halloween poem, with macabre and gruesome references to death, necrophilia, and murder. She laughed it off and thought it was funny. But when she finally met her date in person, there was nothing funny about him. He said things that made her feel creepy at first. Later on in the conversation, she began to feel afraid for her life. In fact, she felt so frightened that she finally excused herself to go to the bathroom, ran out the back door, and never looked back.

6. TOO MANY DETAILS

If someone provides too many tedious details when you ask a simple question or gives away way too much information on her profile or in her communications, it may simply be that she has too much time on her hands. Another possibility is that she is engaging in some creative writing. If she writes in a free-flow, stream-of-consciousness form, you may be able to pick up some unintentionally revealed secrets and even some lies. So pay very close attention to every word you read and keep your eyes peeled for inconsistencies. Likewise, if she puts it all out there and holds nothing back, this may indicate a lack of boundaries and good judgment.

Fake profiles often contain a lot of overly detailed and extremely personal information—not the kind of stuff that people normally reveal when they interact with someone initially. It takes time to get to know personal things about others, so keep that in mind when you see these kinds of profiles online (and you will).

7. CURT RESPONSES OR TOO MANY QUESTIONS

Conversely, if someone's responses are only a few words long and there is minimal communication, he may just be multitasking as he's talking to you. He may be juggling other prospective dates online. Or, he may have something more nefarious to hide. It may just reflect a general lack of interest in you. Most people falter from time to time when they speak, but this shouldn't happen in written communication. If someone is being stingy with information about who he is or what he does, chances are he has something to hide. Likewise, if he pesters you with a lot of questions but doesn't reciprocate when you ask him questions, it is a huge red flag. If he asks you too many questions about your personal or work life, he may be checking you out to see if you know something or someone who could be of use to him.

8. SELF-DEPRECATING COMMENTS SAID IN JEST

If someone tells you she's a "bad girl" in her profile or during her communications with you, believe her. She's actually giving you some very important information about herself, so don't ignore it. Don't bother waiting to find out whether she is correct in her self-assessment. She's not being humble or humorous; she's being honest. Many negative statements followed by "LOL" or "haha" are actual truths that should never be overlooked. If someone makes a threat like "I could just kill myself" or "I could murder you," take it seriously. Even if it is not an actual threat, most normal people don't say things like this or joke around like this with someone they barely know.

9. OVERLY FOCUSED ON FINANCES

Be aware of how often someone refers to money or finances—things being "too expensive," or how he saved money, or how much he makes, as you read his profile and engage in online correspondence. If he seems too focused on money (or the lack thereof), he is telling you about what is uppermost in his mind. If he mentions that he wishes he could afford to do something, or that times are tough or challenging, know that he may be looking for money or for someone to pay or at least share his expenses. If anyone ever asks you for money or tells you quick ways you can make money, know that he/she is looking to get into your wallet or bank account. My advice is to get rid of this person without hesitation.

10. EGOCENTRISM AND NARCISSISM

If every sentence begins with "I," and there is a lot of "me" and "mine" peppered throughout her writing, the number-one priority in her life is likely—guess who?—herself. Another indicator of egocentrism is when someone posts more than a dozen photos of herself. Your only value is as an audience. Likewise, if the conversation is not reciprocal in that she doesn't bother to ask questions about you, doesn't actively listen, and/or dismisses or ignores your comments, you are headed for trouble.

11. POOR SPELLING AND GRAMMAR

While we all make spelling and grammatical mistakes from time to time, a consistent stream of these kinds of errors in someone's writing could indicate issues like dyslexia. This is probably a non-issue for most people, as some of the most intelligent and creative people have been known to be dyslexic. However, this can also reflect a lack of formal education, which is problematic if the person has already indicated he has a college education. If you observe a lot of incorrect verb tenses, this can be a huge telltale sign that you are dealing with a sociopath, as research has recently revealed. (For more on the sociopath, see Chapter 12.)

12. ODD NAMES OR "HANDLES"

The name a person chooses for herself on the Internet or for her email address may be an indication of how she sees herself, how she would like to be seen, and/or what really matters to her. For instance, if her handle or moniker refers to sports, dancing, or traveling, it may reflect an abiding interest in these activities. Likewise, if she uses terms such as "model," "gorgeous," or "hottie," it's safe to assume that she's focused on her looks. It's also very possible that she's misrepresenting her appearance. And certainly, if she uses the terms "athletic" or "big boned" to describe herself, know that she is essentially saying she is overweight, so don't be fooled.

It is interesting to note that many men who have been catfished (more on that later in the chapter) report that the woman claimed she was a model. In fact, during an interview on *20/20*, Nev Schulman, host of the MTV show *Catfish*, says that when someone tells you that he/she is a model, most likely it isn't true.

People who use sexual handles and terminology on nonsexual sites may be focused on finding a sexual partner and uninterested in a long-term relationship. If you read monikers that include words such as *devil, Lucifer, killing, dead, chaos,* or *terror,* or "street" lingo that deals with violence and mayhem, the poster may be revealing some pent-up anger or nefarious thoughts. In that case, you may want to steer clear. Likewise, if someone's handle is different from his real name, he may not be who he says he is. He may be a public person who wants to stay anonymous, or he may be married and living a double life. If you ask about his moniker or tag and he sounds uncomfortable, nervous, or defensive (or worse, refuses to offer any explanation at all), it may be a red flag for you to hit the delete button.

13. IMMEDIATELY BRINGING UP SEX

A lot of people will quickly throw out the bait and start discussing sex and other intimate acts in order to see if you are like-minded. Unless that is what you are after as well, cut her off immediately and change the subject. If she persists, hit delete and block her. People who are sincerely interested in a relationship don't mention sex right off the bat; they take time to get to know you first. Also be aware when a conversation suddenly takes a turn toward sex, and it sounds as though you may be headed for phone or cyber sex. This may be the other person's way of sexually gratifying or amusing himself at your expense, so don't allow yourself to be exploited in this way. And (this should go without saying)—*never, ever allow anyone to convince you to send provocative or nude photos of yourself under any circumstances.* He may use it against you to extort money from you or end up ruining your reputation.

One innocent teenager was victimized by an online "suitor" who pressured her into sending a topless photo of herself. The suitor, who turned out to be another female student, made her life a living hell as she shared the compromising photo with all of her friends. As a result, the victim developed a bad reputation at school, and was so tormented by cyber bullies that she ended up killing herself. This horrible scenario happens all the time and regularly ruins young people's lives. (Incidentally, it is also a crime to send or receive naked photos online if you are underage.) So, parents must monitor their children's online communications and stress that they must never send nude photos of themselves online, as it is a crime for which they will suffer consequences that are out of the parents' control.

14. GUILT TRIPS

When someone leverages guilt tactics to make you feel badly for not responding to her, not responding quickly enough, or not making contact more often, she is attempting to gain emotional control over you so that she can better manipulate you. All too often, well-meaning and thoughtful people fall for this ploy because they don't want to hurt anyone's feelings and/or they have a strong need to be liked. Don't make that mistake. If *anyone*, especially someone you don't know or someone whom you are just getting to know, admonishes you online or tries to guilt trip you, hit the delete button and block her as soon as possible.

15. PHOTOS THAT LIE

Always take note of the background and surroundings when you look at someone's photo. Someone who has given you the impression that he has money, but then sends you a photo of himself in a sparsely or poorly furnished home, may be lying to you. Someone who tells you he doesn't have kids, but sends you a photo of himself with a baby carrier in the background or kid's toys in his living room, may be a married man looking for a little fun on the side.

If a man posts photos with other women who are not family members or vice versa, it may mean that he is already in a relationship (or relationships). Or, it could be his way of not-so-subtly broadcasting the type of person he finds attractive. Someone like this is basically saying, If you aren't as pretty as the women in my photos, don't waste your time. If he is half-naked or the photos are provocative in any way, having you as a sex partner is first and foremost on his mind. If he has no photo at all, he may be arrogant, high profile, or have something to hide. He may also have low self-esteem and thus doesn't feel physically attractive enough to post his photo.

If the photo looks too professional, if he is *too* good looking, or if he doesn't post any candid shots, be careful. That photo may not be of him at all. As well, paying close attention to how someone is dressed (style of clothing, trends from a certain time period, etc.) can give you a clue as to the relative age of the posted photo—and the poster.

ON CATFISHING AND BEING CATFISHED

Richard Perry is a famous Hollywood record producer. He produced award-winning albums for many pop stars for decades, including Rod Stewart. Presently he is also Jane Fonda's boyfriend and companion. But years before Jane Fonda came into his life, this very bright and talented producer was pursued by a woman who wasn't who she claimed to be. Miranda Grosvenor told Richard that she was a blond Tulane University student, a wealthy socialite, and an international model from Louisiana. What Richard didn't know was that Miranda was telling other rich, powerful, and famous men the same thing—men like Warren Beatty, Bono, Bob Dylan, Ted Kennedy, Robert De Niro, Rush Limbaugh, Richard Gere, and Billy Joel.

According to a *Vanity Fair* article, Richard Perry was so enamored with her that he proposed marriage even though they had never met:

> *I used to come home from ...working in the recording studio....*
> *I would pour myself a glass of wine and have dinner in front of the*
> *speakerphone with Miranda and we'd talk for hours.... I wasn't [go-*
> *ing to] let it go any further without meeting her. So I demanded that*
> *she come to New York. I was anxious. Especially when I met her in*
> *her hotel room. And she wanted ... all the lights to be out.*

When Richard Perry's eyes finally adjusted to the darkness in the hotel room, he didn't see the beautiful, blond, 23-year-old bombshell model he expected. Instead, he saw an overweight, physically unattractive woman with a large mole on her face. Richard ended his relationship with Miranda Grosvenor, whose real name turned out to be Whitney Walton. Apparently she was a lonely and bored Baton Rouge social worker whose hobby was seducing wealthy, powerful men through her alluring voice and conversational skills.

This happened in 1999, when there was no term to describe the phenomenon of someone pretending to be someone else and emotionally seducing others to become romantically involved. Today this phenomenon is called *catfishing*. Richard Perry was *catfished* via phone, but today, most catfishing takes place online. The term "catfish" comes from the eponymous 2010 documentary film by Nev Schulman. Nev, a photographer, was sent a painting of one of his previously published pictures by an 8-year-old Midwestern child prodigy artist named Abby. They became Facebook friends, and Abby's family (her mom, Angela, dad, and beautiful and talented half-sister, Megan) joined his network soon thereafter. Nev embarked on a long-distance online and phone relationship with the older sister, Megan.

The two eventually agreed to meet at some point. But Nev's suspicions began to arise when he discovered that MP3s she sent him, which Megan claimed were her songs, were actually taken from someone else's YouTube performances. Nev uncovered other false claims and was devastated. But for the sake of continuing his documentary on finding love on the Internet, he took his brother and a friend along on a car trip in order to make an unannounced visit to Megan.

Nev ultimately discovered that Megan's mom, Angela, was in reality a frumpy, married, middle-aged woman whose life consisted solely of caring for two severely disabled twin stepsons. She was the one who created the paintings and sent them to Nev, not young Abby. It turned out that Abby was not an artist at all; in fact, when Nev met the little girl and asked her about her art skills, she had no idea what he was talking about. Angela did turn out to have an older daughter, but her name was not Megan. Her real daughter had actually been estranged from Angela for a long time. Clearly Megan was not the young woman in the photos Nev received; it was all part of a ruse to make him think he was in a relationship with a young, beautiful woman from Washington. The photos of "Megan" had been lifted off the Internet. When Angela finally admitted to her lies, she claimed that she had been acting out a fantasy of what her life might have been like had she not made the choices she did.

The actual term "catfished" came about after Nev spoke to Angela's real-life husband, Vince, who said that when live cod are shipped from Asia to North America, fish that remain inactive in the tanks become fleshy and mushy. To prevent this, fishermen put a catfish in with the live cod to keep them active. Vince told Nev that he believed that people like his wife are essentially "catfish" who keep people running in circles—hence the term meaning those who figuratively give others the runaround. The term has become even more popular since Nev created a television show for MTV called *Catfish*, which he also currently hosts. The show focuses on the truth and lies in the lives of those who have been involved in an online relationship.

Being catfished can happen to anyone who is vulnerable, lonely, and looking for love. I met a once-famous and attractive comedic actress after she had become middle-aged and less attractive, and gone through several divorces and scores of bad relationships with men. One day she called to tell me she had finally found the love of her life—a man she had met on Facebook. He was an Italian model who was in his mid-30s and came from a wealthy family. She said he was not only gorgeous, but also the most romantic man she had ever encountered. He sent her his favorite music, beautiful poetry, and photos of roses with romantic sayings on a daily basis. She even told me how they had sexy chats over the computer on IM (Instant Messenger). She was especially excited because he was planning to send her a ticket to visit him in Italy, where he was going to take her on his yacht and to watch him play polo.

When she finally showed me the photos of his yacht and his polo pony, my suspicions were aroused—mostly because neither he nor anyone else was on his yacht or near his beloved, prized polo pony. To me, they looked like generic photos that anyone could grab off the Internet. But when I saw "Giovanni's" photos, however, I knew the jig was up. I loudly and involuntarily yelled out, "Oh my God!"

"See? I told you he was gorgeous!" she chimed in.

"I hate to be the bearer of bad news," I said pityingly, "but these are photos of Gabriel Aubrey, the Canadian model who also happens to be the father of Halle Berry's child. My dear, you have been played!"

Needless to say, the former actress was shocked and embarrassed. None of her other friends had mentioned to her who the man in the photos really was. Perhaps they really didn't know, or maybe they just lied to her by omission. I, on the other hand, chose to tell her the truth.

Notre Dame's talented football star Manti Te'o was also embarrassed from being catfished, especially when the truth was finally revealed all over the media. Apparently this young man had been emotionally involved in an online romance with a girl named Lennay Kekua for years. Manti tried to meet her on several occasions, but she would always cancel on him at the last minute. Unfortunately she passed away before they had the chance to meet in person.

Initially, Manti was too naïve and too focused on his football playing and schooling to realize he was being scammed. He was also emotionally invested in Lennay. Even when she said she had been in a car accident and was in the hospital, he still never suspected she was anything but who she said she was. After all, when he stayed on the phone with her every night she was in the hospital, he could hear her breathing. Manti later told reporters that he remained on the phone with Lennay all night because she told him the only thing that would help her sleep and recover was if he stayed on the phone with her, and so naturally he obliged.

One day, Manti received a phone call from someone claiming to be Lennay's family spokesperson, saying that Lennay had died. He was told not to attend her funeral because Lennay's mom didn't want him there. Manti agreed, because he really didn't want the first and only time that he would see Lennay to be when she was lying in her coffin. Even though he never met her in person, he was still emotionally devastated by the loss. It was only when Manti received a phone call from a woman who sounded exactly like Lennay, saying "Manti, it's me," three months *after* Lennay had passed away, that he realized he had been catfished.

When he finally discovered that this woman was fictitious and that he had been played, Manti didn't want anyone to think he was crazy for having fallen in love with a woman he had never met. So he lied to his own father and to his friends that he had actually had a physical relationship with Lennay, and that he had met her in person well before she passed away. Manti became the liar. He was too embarrassed to tell the truth about how he had been fooled, so he lied to family, friends, and journalists about his relationship with this fictional girlfriend.

Manti finally publicly admitted what had happened to him. Apparently, a man named Ronaiah Tuiasosopo openly confessed that he and another man and a woman were responsible for the entire hoax. Ronaiah even went on the *Dr. Phil Show* to do a *mea culpa*, in which he apologized and discussed the possibility that he might be gay and in love with Manti Te'o.

The moral of this story is this: in dealing with any online or phone relationship, *meet the person right away*. If that is not logistically or financially possible, get on Skype immediately and make sure you see the whites of his eyes. If he comes up with excuses and cancels, it is a huge warning sign that you should then cancel any further involvement with him. Remember that being catfished can happen to anyone, regardless of wealth, talent, intelligence, or fame.

IF IT DOESN'T LOOK RIGHT OR READ RIGHT...IT'S NOT RIGHT!

If something doesn't look right or read right, chances are, *something isn't right*. Don't second guess what you read or see over the Internet or try to interpret it in a different, more positive light. Take what you read and see online as it is, not as what you want it to be. Above all, learn to trust your instincts, as you will learn in the next chapter.

PART II
HUMAN LIE DETECTION

This section will stress the importance of trusting your instincts as you learn how to listen to the little signals in your own body, signals that are alerting you that something is wrong. You will discover the importance of context in assessing whether a person is lying, or whether there is some other, more benign underlying cause for the suspect body language movement and vocal cues.

You will discover the Profile of a Liar. You will learn how to dissect the four components of the liar's communication: facial language, body language, voice patterns, and speech patterns. And finally, you will observe the specific visual signals (face and body movements) of familiar newsmakers at the moment of their deception. You'll also read detailed descriptions of what they said and how they said it. This is designed to etch these specific signals of deception into your memory, so that you can easily recognize them when you observe the same signs in others.

CHAPTER 6
INSTINCTS AND CONTEXT

Larissa always dreamed of having her own radio talk show. She met Steve, who claimed to be in the entertainment industry and know a lot about the radio business. He told her that with all the contacts he had, he could get her a real radio show in a lot of markets in no time. He told her to not waste her time doing a free Internet radio show because he could guarantee that she would make $100,000 during her first year under his management. All she had to do was give him $2,000 so he could make her a demo tape, make some calls, and travel to meetings on her behalf.

While a part of her was excited, the other part of her said "no way." Plus, something about him repulsed her. Morbidly obese, with excess skin hanging from his neck and a misshaped, shaved head, Steve was not the most physically attractive man. But there was something more about Steve that told her to keep her away, something that something wasn't quite right about him. But she dismissed those inner feelings and even chastised herself for being superficial about his unappealing looks.

Had she known about body language "tells," she would have been much more conscious (and leery) of his clammy handshake, slow and deliberate movements, boring, monotonous drone, and lack of eye contact. She might have known that these were all potential signs of a liar. Larissa's senses were picking up information about Steve, and her limbic system, deep inside her brain, was translating that data into emotions and gut feelings. These negative feelings were then reflected in or expressed by her body, in the form of a sudden, rapid heartbeat, a flushed face, and stomach pains. When Larissa dismissed what her body was telling her about Steve, she paid the price by becoming $2,000 poorer. When she discovered that she had been scammed by this con artist, she wanted to kick herself for not heeding her initial instincts. She knew she had been conned when Steve constantly gave her excuses and lied about promised meetings he never intended to arrange. She could never get him on the phone, and, ultimately, he changed his number.

Unsurprisingly, Larissa wasn't Steve's only victim. By happenstance she met Kari, another woman whom he had scammed years earlier. Kari, in turn, told her about four *other* women who had fallen prey to Steve. Larissa was lucky she only lost $2,000, as the others had lost a lot more than that. The message here is *always trust your instincts*. Your instincts always have your best interests at heart, and they are almost always right. Never ignore a twinge in your stomach, a sudden sinking feeling, or any other bodily signal that screams (or whispers), *No, don't do it*.

Direct your attention to any immediate physical changes in your body and whatever negative emotion(s) you are feeling. Try to define the exact emotion(s) you are experiencing. Don't ignore or deny those alarm bells by second guessing yourself, by thinking you are being too judgmental, or by projecting positive traits that don't exist onto other people. This may be wishful thinking on your part, seeing people people as you want them to be, not as they really are.

ARE YOU REALLY LOOKING AND LISTENING?

If something sounds like a lie, or someone looks as though they are lying, chances are there is deception going on. However, before you can assess whether someone is lying, you must stop, look, and listen, just as you do before you walk across the street so as to avoid oncoming cars. The same holds true when you look for the signs that someone isn't being truthful.

You must pay close attention to peoples' faces when you speak to them and ask questions. You must carefully watch for signals that they may be lying. Likewise you should pay close attention to their body language and body movements, as that too can give you information as to whether someone is telling the truth. Next you have to listen carefully to the tone of voice, speech patterns, and of course the content of what is actually being said.

CONTEXT IS KEY

Let's say that your boyfriend, Jack, is constantly tugging at his nose and scratching his skin as he tells you about his new dog. You realize that nose pulling and scratching can be signs of deception, but Jack may not be lying at all. Everything Jack says and does has to be assessed in the proper context. And the first thing to consider when evaluating context is the *base-line*—that is, how someone acts when he or she is telling the truth. Once you've established this, everything he or she says and does can be evaluated against this baseline of normalcy.

Jack may be tugging at his nose and scratching his arms not because he is lying, but because he has allergies. Another possibility is that talking about his dog is eliciting anxiety in him. Upon further inquiry, you learn that Jack's dog is a puppy, and after receiving a few puppy nips himself, Jack is worried about the puppy biting his kids or the neighbor's kids.

On the other hand, let's say that you've never noticed Jack scratching himself or pulling on his nose before. Let's say you ask him where he was last night. All of a sudden you see him pull on his nose as he tells you he was at his friend Joe's house. You notice him scratching himself as he tells you an elaborate story of what they did last night, filed with many tangents and too much information. Now his nose tugs and arm-scratching may be telling you something different. He may not have been with Joe until the wee hours of the morning at all. Instead, he may have been with another woman.

So the context of a person's statements and actions—specifically, his or her baseline—is key in deciphering a lie.

When cyclist Lance Armstrong was asked about his twins and his family during interviews, he never pursed his lips together, pointed his finger, or exhibited a defensive tone. But when the tone of the interview changed, and he was bluntly asked if he ever "doped" or used drugs during a race, his pursed lips, finger-pointing, and defensive tone spoke volumes. This is another perfect example of how someone's baseline can inform your intuition that you are being lied to.

CHAPTER 7

THE BODY LANGUAGE OF A LIAR

When you analyze the body language of a liar, you need to carefully observe all of the changes and movements in his or her breathing, skin, posture, position or stance, arms, hands, and feet. In this chapter you will discover the specific body language "tells" that may reveal that someone is being dishonest.

BREATHING CHANGES

Often the first thing you will notice when someone lies is a change in his or her breathing. When people are calm and relaxed, they will usually breathe in such a way that you'll be able to see their abdomen moving up and down as the air goes in and out of their lungs; the abdomen rises upon inhaling, and flattens out upon exhaling. But when someone is lying, or at least showing signs of deception, he/she will often breathe in such a way that instead of seeing the abdomen moving up and down, you'll see his/her upper chest and shoulders rise and fall.

Photo 7-1: Lance Armstrong during his Oprah interview, showing tenseness in his shoulders and upper chest breathing. Photo credit: Getty Images Entertainment.

Oftentimes there is visible tension in the upper chest area, indicating anxiety. This was most evident in the interview that Armstrong gave when he admitted to Oprah Winfrey that he had engaged in doping. While he appeared forthright in many of the things he revealed, from time to time you could observe a visible tenseness in his shoulders as he breathed. These may have been times when he was not being completely truthful as he fielded Oprah's penetrating questions.

When someone is engaged in deception, you will often see him suddenly puff out his cheeks as he exhales. What he is doing is oxygenating himself. His autonomic nervous system is working overtime because of a sudden buildup of carbon dioxide in his system. Therefore, he immediately draws a large breath and then blows it out in order to regain equilibrium. This helps the liar regain his composure as he releases the buildup of tension caused by the lying. Thus this blowing out of air is often a huge "tell" when it comes to detecting a liar.

Photo 7-2: O.J. Simpson forcefully blowing out air through his mouth during his Las Vegas trial for burglary, robbery, and assault. Photo credit: Daniel Gluskoter, Splash News.

Here we see a photo of O.J. Simpson in court during the second day of jury selection for his 2008 trial for burglary, robbery, and assault, at the Clark County Regional Justice Center in Las Vegas. Notice how his chest is raised and expanded as he fills his lungs with air, and his cheeks puffed out as he prepares to release a sudden burst of air in order to release what was most likely overwhelming stress and tension. This photo was taken the day a jury of his peers was being selected.

Based on his past experiences in the courtroom, during both his criminal and his civil trials for the deaths of Nicole Simpson and Ron Goldman, Simpson was likely well aware of the importance of picking a jury in terms of the outcome of the trial. His sudden upper chest breathing and intense burst of air illustrate the stress he was most likely experiencing during the jury selection process.

SKIN CHANGES

When people lie you can often observe changes in their skin, in terms of the color of the skin and the presence of perspiration. In lighter-skinned people, the skin may become flushed, red, or blotchy. Usually the redness can be seen on the cheeks and nose, but may also appear uniformly over the entire face, from the forehead to the neck, as well as on the ears. The redness or blushing can range from a light pink to a very dark red. This color change is the result of an increase in adrenalin and the concurrent changes in the blood vessels and capillaries. In darker-skinned people, the skin can become paler or ashier.

Photo 7-3: Former Senator and Presidential candidate John Edwards blushing and perspiring (two signals of deception)—and even smiling—in his mug shot. Photo credit: Splash News.

Here we can see disgraced former Senator and Presidential candidate John Edwards' mug shot photo, after he was arrested for finance fraud. The lie he is telling in this photo is that he is happy and that all is well. Even though his lips are smiling, it is very much a fake smile (more about the fake smile in Chapter 8). His "happiness" is also belied by the darkened and blotchy or mottled skin on his face and the sides of his neck. (In the original color photo, the blush is much more obvious, with his face an assertive pinkish-red.)

Photo 7-4: Lance Armstrong showing sudden darkening (reddening, in the original photo) in skin color on his nose, cheeks, neck, and ears as he is asked a question about his doping. Photo credit: Jennifer Lorenzini/Splash News.

You may also see redness on a liar's ears, nose, and cheeks when he feels that his lie is about to be revealed. Even though Lance Armstrong's skin was normally tan, the contrasting redness on his ears, sides of his neck, nose, and even his mouth during the interview revealed the sudden change in his autonomic nervous system and the resultant increased blood flow. Along with a flushed color, veins may suddenly appear on the forehead, as they too enlarge due to the increased blood pressure and flow.

Sweat

Perspiration on the face may also indicate deception. Sweat will often break out on the forehead, nose, cheeks, chin, and upper lip. In the photo of John Edwards, you can see the visible breakout of perspiration on his face as he puts on a happy face for his mug shot. Facial sweat is the result of the body generating heat, which also accounts for the concurrent redness and blushing. In the body's attempt to cool down, sweat is released through the pores of the body and the face.

Photo 7-5: Perspiration can be seen over President Clinton's upper lip, forehead, cheeks, and sides of his nose as he lies to the American people about his affair with Monica Lewinsky. Photo credit: Joyce Naltchayan/Getty Images.

But since the upper lip muscles usually tense up during deception, it is not uncommon to see beads of sweat actually accumulating in this area. This is often a clear giveaway that the person is lying. While we all noticed Clinton's angry finger-pointing, few were able to get close enough to see that he was also sweating profusely as he spoke. If you look closely at this photo, you can actually see little beads of perspiration and shininess over his upper lip.

President Clinton was not the only one who sweated it out as he lied. Even when Armstrong wasn't out riding his bike, he was still doing a lot of sweating during his interviews. As early as 2006, in his ESPN.com interview for *Outside the Lines*, the perspiration beads over his upper lip were clearly visible throughout the entirety of the interview as he blatantly lied about not taking performance-enhancing drugs.

This telltale signal of upper-lip sweat was also what alerted the suspicions of U.S. Customs inspector Diana Dean regarding Ahmed Ressam, a.k.a. the "Millenium Bomber." Ressam tried to enter the United States from Canada on December of 1999, driving a car that contained the makings of a bomb. As he left the ferry from British Columbia to Port Angeles, Washington, inspector Dean conducted her routine questioning, as she did with all passengers. What gave her cause for concern was seeing Ressam's upper lip break out in beads of sweat. She immediately called on her fellow officers to search Ressam's car, where the raw materials for bomb-making were discovered. If she had not noticed Ressam's sweating, there could have been a very serious terrorist attack on U.S. soil.

POSTURE CHANGES

When people engage in deception, you will notice sudden changes in their posture. Often their posture will stiffen up, and both shoulders will become rigid and roll forward. Their head may also droop down in a slight forward movement. According to Los Angeles Police Reports, in February 2009, before they were to attend a Grammy Awards celebration, Rapper Chris Brown assualted his girlfriend, Rihanna Fenty, after he tried to push her out of his car. He was subsequently arrested on domestic violence charges. When he went to court in April 2009, even though he pleaded Not Guilty to his crime, his body language suggested that he was feeling very guilty, indeed.

The normally square-shouldered and cocky Chris Brown looked anything but when he appeared before the judge in a Los Angeles courtroom. His shoulders suddenly hunched over and he bowed his head and looked down, as you can see in the photo on the following page. His posture fairly screamed "shame" and "guilt."

A similar postural change could be observed the exact moment Notre Dame football star Manti Te'o lied as he talked about his nonexistent girlfriend before the scandal broke. As he spoke to Kate Sullivan of WBBM, a CBS affiliate in Chicago, you can see his posture tensing up and his shoulders rise up in a tense shrug. Even though he claimed he had nothing

Photo 7-6: Chris Brown pleading Not Guilty as his posture belies his innocence. In a plea deal to get probation, he ended up pleading Guilty for abusing Rihanna. Photo credit: Pooled Pictures/Splash News.

to do with the hoax, his posture, with rounded shoulders and head bowed forward and down in a turtle-like position, indicated that he was likely still being deceptive. He was most likely continuing to lie about his non-existent, dead girlfriend, even after the hoax had been exposed. His body language also reflected his shame in being caught in his lies.

One of the reasons liars will assume this quasi–fetal position is because they are feeling emotionally vulnerable and/or embarrassed. Therefore, they literally minimize themselves by taking up less space, reflecting that they are feeling "small" emotionally. It is also the body's instinctive way of protecting itself. So when you suddenly catch a person in a lie, you will often see a hunched over, turtle-like fetal position similar to the postural change. We saw this when Barry Bonds was caught lying by omission at a press conference. While he was taciturn on the subject of his steroid use, his protective body language spoke volumes.

You can also see this hunched-over posture in John Edwards' mug shot. Usually Edwards' posture was ramrod straight, with his shoulders back and head held high as he brimmed with self-confidence. But in his mug shot we see that his shoulders are rounded and pulled forward. This is the body language of shame and sadness. So his body is actually telling us the truth—that Edwards is not happy at all, but instead feeling shame and distress about his arrest for campaign fraud.

Photo 7-7: Former Presidential candidate John Edwards with hunched-over shoulders in his mug shot. Photo credit: Splash News.

When someone loses self-confidence you can often see his or her posture change into this hunched-over fetal position. This is particularly evident when you see someone who is convicted of a crime go from a ramrod straight, cocky posture, complete with a self-assured swagger when he walks, to a hunched-over, turtle-like posture with head bowed, as he begins to realize that he will not be getting away with his crime. When Penn State football coach Jerry Sandusky was first accused of child molestation, his straight posture and upright head position shouted to the world that he was confident nothing would happen to him, and that he would simply shake loose all of the allegations against him. But as time passed, and more and more people came forward with their claims, Sandusky's once-erect posture became more and more hunched over and turtle-like. His feelings of guilt (or at least his anxiety over being caught) must have been almost unbearable as he realized that he would have to face the consequences for his egregious actions. In the most recent videos and photos taken of him attending a post-sentencing hearing (about a possible re-trial, which was denied), even though he still proclaimed his innocence, his body language and posture of guilt and defeat belied his claim.

This turtle-like postural change is also often a telltale sign for law enforcement officers when they are questioning suspects. They know to become more direct and probe more deeply with their questioning.

Shrugging it off

When someone suddenly shrugs his shoulders when speaking about a critical issue or answering a pointed question, chances are he may be lying to you. Former Major League baseball player Barry Bonds often shrugged his shoulders during press conferences, as he refused to answer questions (lying by omission) posed to him by reporters concerning his steroid usage. Lying to the wrong people—Federal prosecutors, for starters—resulted in Bonds being indicted on four counts of perjury and one count of obstruction of justice in a government investigation. He was convicted on the latter count in 2011 for giving an evasive answer to a question under oath. Because of his lies, he was also denied entry into the Baseball Hall of Fame.

Another person whose lying was all-too-evident in a courtroom was O. J. Simpson. At his sentencing hearing in a Las Vegas courtroom, O.J. Simpson stood up in his shackles and offered an apology for what he did. As he did so, he tilted his head to one side and shrugged his shoulders, as you can see in the photo. This indicates that his apology was likely anything but sincere. Specifically, he shrugged his shoulders as he said, "I didn't want to hurt any of these guys." This belied the fact that his intention was indeed to "hurt these guys," as he came into their hotel room with a gun in order to retrieve what he saw as his property.

The presiding judge, Judge Jackie Glass, clearly saw through O.J.'s "apology" for what it was: deception and manipulation in hopes of receiving a lighter sentence. She rejected his apology out of hand and said that what he did was "much more than stupidity." She ended up sentencing him to 15 years in prison.

Photo 7-8: O.J. Simpson shrugging his shoulders as he gave his apology during his sentencing hearing. Copyright: Getty Images.

Backing up

When people realize they've been caught in a lie, sometimes their entire body will suddenly, automatically, and uncontrollably jerk backward. The liar has literally been "taken aback" that his deception was uncovered.

The liar's back is literally "against the wall" as he makes a sudden, slight jump or jerk backward. In doing so, the posture quickly becomes both rigid and erect. There is also visible tension in the neck and shoulders, as you can see in the photo of O.J. Simpson, taken during one of his most revealing interviews, given on the 10-year anniversary of his wife's murder. We see him literally backing up as Catherine Crier's question clearly strikes a nerve.

Photo 7-9: O.J. Simpson literally taken aback by a question posed to him during his interview with Catherine Crier. Photo Credit: AdLIB Design/Splash News.

Leaning forward

People who lie want desperately to be believed. Therefore, in their desperation, they will lean into the person they are talking to as a means of ingratiating themselves and appearing affable and likeable. It's basically a manipulative attempt to entice others into believing them. As a result, you may often see them lean forward when they are engaged in one-on-one communication. It is an attempt to create a false sense of intimacy and make you think they are telling you the truth. The photo on the following page captured the only time O.J. leaned forward during the entire interview; it was likely an attempt to drive home the point that he was not involved in his wife's death. In my opinion, this sudden leaning forward, combined with the finger-pointing, appear to indicate deception.

Photo 7-10: O.J. leaning forward during a Court TV interview with Catherine Crier on the 10-year anniversary of his wife's murder. Photo Credit: AdLIB Design/Splash News.

We can often see this behavior in criminals who are interviewed prior to their conviction. When Scott Peterson was interviewed by Diane Sawyer, we could see him leaning forward throughout the whole interview, likely in a feeble attempt to appear ingratiating and believable. He gave this interview before his wife Laci's remains were found along with those of their unborn child. As he leaned forward, he continued to lie about not knowing the whereabouts of his pregnant wife, when all along he knew that her body was at the bottom of the bay. Peterson did this with another interviewer on CBS, as well. Even though the journalist confronted him about his lies regarding his girlfriend, Amber Frey, Peterson still remained in that forward-leaning position.

We also observed this posture with convicted wife-killer Drew Peterson on the *Today Show*, as he tried to convince Matt Lauer and the world that he had nothing to do with the death of his third wife, Kathleen Savio, or the disappearance of his fourth wife, Stacy. We also saw it with convicted boyfriend-killer Jodi Arias as she spoke to *48 Hours* and tried to come across as a sweet and likeable girl, even though she knew that she had killed him by stabbing him multiples times in the shower. Another common thread with each of these forward-leaning criminals is that they rarely, if ever, move from this position during their interviews.

Former Presidential candidate John Edwards leaned forward like this during his interview with ABC reporter Bob Woodruff, as he denied that he was the father of his mistress, Rielle Hunter's child.

FIDGETING OR STAYING TOO STILL

Another telltale signal of deception is fidgeting. The reason for this is that the autonomic nervous system is once again taking over in a primitive "fight-or-flight" response. Oftentimes people will want to literally flee from stressful or uncomfortable situations. So if a liar knows he is going to be interrogated or interviewed, the innate biological instinct kicks in to physically get him out of there—hence, the excess energy and extraneous body movements.

On the other hand, a liar may not move at all. This may be a sign of the primitive neurological "fight," rather than the "flight," response, as the body positions and readies itself for possible confrontation. When you speak and engage in normal conversation, it is natural to move your body around in subtle, relaxed, and, for most part, unconscious movements. So if you observe a rigid and catatonic stance devoid of movement, it is often a huge warning sign that something is off. At the very least, this person is trying too hard to keep control over himself and his conversation; at most, he may be trying to manipulate and deceive you. This very same thing could be observed in the body language of convicted wife killer Drew Peterson. In his many interviews, he would sit rigid and stone faced as he proclaimed his innocence. He insisted he was innocent of his third wife, Kathleen Savio's murder, and insisted he knew nothing of the whereabouts of his fourth wife, Stacy, who had suddenly disappeared. With his hands firmly clasped in front of him, Peterson never moved from that position.

When a suspect is being interrogated by law enforcement and seems rooted to the spot, it is usually taken as a red flag that the suspect knows a lot more than he's letting on. Further, if he's gripping his arms or hands, he is literally attempting to "get a grip" on himself so he won't reveal what he wants or needs to keep secret.

Photo 7-11: Nicki Minaj (far right) exhibiting a fixed body position, with clasped hands and crossed arms over her knee, throughout the entire panel discussion as she tries to conceal what were most likely negative feelings toward her fellow judge Mariah Carey (far left). Photo credit: Getty News Entertainment.

Nicki Minaj consistently and vociferously denied being involved in a feud with her fellow judge, singer Mariah Carey. However, the fact that Nicki sat rigid and immobile and refused to even look at Mariah, spoke volumes about the truth concerning this feud. This unnatural behavior is usually a red flag as far as deception is concerned, precisely because it *is* unnatural. The liar attempts to micromanage her body movements so that no one will think she's lying; ironically, however, it is this very behavior that is letting people know that she is in all probability being deceitful.

CHANGES IN HEAD POSITION

When someone has been caught in a lie, you will often see various odd or awkward head movements. The head will be (a) retracted or jerked back, (b) bowed down, or (c) cocked or tilted to one side. If you see someone suddenly make any of these movements, particularly after you have asked him a pointed question, it's possible he's not being completely honest with you.

The head jerk

We often saw the sudden head jerk during death row inmate Scott Peterson's trial for the murder of his wife and unborn son. His head would suddenly move backward when he heard something in the courtroom that pointed to the truth about his involvement in their deaths. You can see this in the following photo of O.J. Simpson during his interview with Catherine Crier. The timing of the photo is important: he jerks his head back just as he begins to respond to a significant question regarding Nicole's murder. This sudden head movement is often an indication that someone is not telling the truth.

Photo 7-12: O.J. Simpson during his Catherine Crier interview on Court TV. This is the moment he suddenly jerks his head back as he answers a question.
Photo credit: AdLIB Designs/Splash News.

Next we have a photo of Lance Armstrong as he's asked an unexpected question about his doping. Note the position of his head and how far back it has retreated as he processes the question. Anytime you see someone's head suddenly jerk back when they lie, are caught or think they may be caught in a lie, or hear something that might uncover their lie—this sudden, awkward, and very obvious movement speaks volumes.

Photo 7-13: Dramatic example of a head jerk. The photo was taken during an interview on a panel in 2009, as Armstrong was asked a question about his doping. Photo Credit: Jennifer Lorenzini/Splash News.

The head bow

When someone with a conscience is caught in a lie or hears an unpleasant truth, he/she will often automatically bow his/her head. This is often a sign or contrition or shame. When Tiger Woods called a press conference in 2010 in order to "apologize" for his cheating, his head was bowed almost the entire time. You can also see this kind of body language in young children, after you ask them to come clean about something you know they did. When you see the bowed head, they are letting you know that they are ashamed they got caught and that they did indeed do something they were not supposed to do.

With his head is slightly bowed, singer and rapper Chris Brown pleaded Not Guilty to his charges of domestic violence against his girlfriend, singer Rihanna. He of course knew this plea was a lie and that he was guilty of pummeling her on the night of the Grammy Awards.

Photo 7-14: Chris Brown with his head slightly bowed as he pleads Not Guilty for a crime he knows he committed, and which he admitted to in a subsequent hearing. His bowed head may also reflect shame over the incident. Photo credit: Pooled Pictures/Splash News.

The head cock or tilt

When you see someone suddenly cock his head or tilt it to one side, it often indicates uncertainty. This can often be seen when people are asked pointed questions or when their lie has been revealed. It is the body's immediate, unconscious way of saying, *I'm not sure how to answer this question because I may have to manufacture a lie.* When Drew Peterson was asked directly about his involvement in the disappearance of his fourth wife, the normally stiff postured ex-policeman immediately cocked his head to the side as he denied any involvement in her disappearance. This may have been a red flag indicating possible deception. Obviously the particular question struck a nerve, or Drew likely would not have presented with this faux-quizzical attitude.

Lance Armstrong cocked his head to the side as he was called to the stage in 2010 during the closing ceremonies of the Tour de France. In his case this was most likely a clear signal of deception. As questions were hurled at him during the spontaneous press conference, he probably wasn't sure how to couch his lie. He knew he didn't deserve the glowing accolades that were being tossed at his feet. He knew he had attained the highest award in cycling by cheating.

Photo 7-15: Lance Armstrong cocking his head to one side during his Oprah Winfrey interview, indicating possible deception by commission or omission.
Photo credit: Getty News Entertainment.

In my opinion, Lance Armstrong was still lying even when he finally admitted to using performance-enhancing drugs to win tournaments. His body language (in particular, the cocked head) led me to believe that there was a lot more he was not revealing and may even have been lying about outright.

Photo 7-16: O.J. Simpson with his head tilted to one side during a sentencing hearing in a Las Vegas courtroom. Photo credit: Pool/Getty Images News.

Here we see O.J. Simpson apologizing to the court and to Judge Jackie Glass for his actions. It was clear from his body language—specifically, the quizzical head tilt—that O.J. didn't believe one word of his apology. The position of his head was one of the signals that gave away his disingenuousness as he spoke.

Neck touching

As we already discussed in the previous section, the neck is an eminently vulnerable part of the human body. The throat houses the anatomical mechanisms that enable us to eat, speak, and breathe—activities necessary to life.

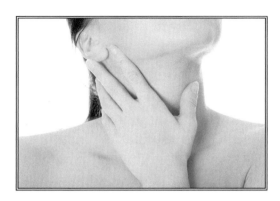

Photo 7-17: Covering the throat with the hand
is often a big "tell" of deception. Photo credit:
Piotr Marcinski, Shutterstock, Inc.

When people cover their throat with their hand, it is often an automatic, uncontrollable protective gesture indicating vulnerability. Sometimes this feeling of vulnerability is a natural result of lying. We often see this when someone has been busted after telling a lie. This is also a common reaction when someone is accused of something, whether directly or indirectly. I have often seen this in the courtroom when I work as a consultant for attorneys. I can always tell when someone's testimony has hit a nerve with the defendant, when I see his or her hand covering the front of his/her throat. Law enforcement officers often watch for this throat-touching signal when they interrogate a suspect, as it can be a sign of deception. Even though the suspect may claim otherwise, this gesture speaks loudly as to his/her knowledge of and/or involvement in the crime.

Famed actor Al Pacino recently posed for a publicity portrait announcing his title role in the forthcoming Joe Paterno biopic. In this very rare photo, Al Pacino was photographed not in character, but as himself; interestingly, he is covering his throat with his hand. For decades it has been well-known in the entertainment industry that Al Pacino is loathe to do publicity because he is an intensely private man. Thus, it is understandable why he might have felt he was being duplicitous or at least disingenuous by fulfilling a contractual obligation to engage in public relations for an upcoming film. His pose, with his hand covering his neck, also may reflect his discomfort and vulnerability, in addition to possible deception.

Collar and neck tugging or scratching

When people tug at the collar of their shirt or the side of their neck, or suddenly loosen their tie, it may indicate deception or anger over hearing an uncomfortable truth. Someone like this is literally getting "hot under the collar" as his autonomic system goes into high gear, thereby increasing his body temperature. This is why liars often feel a sudden surge of heat; when this happens, you will often see them loosen their collar, or scratch or pull at their throat or neck area.

Photo 7-18: Loosening the collar and tie is often a signal of deception, as the liar literally gets "hot under the collar." Photo credit: David Stuart Productions/Shutterstock, Inc.

This gesture may also be a reaction to extreme stress or to having one's lie exposed. We often saw O.J. Simpson tugging on his collar during his Las Vegas robbery trial, particularly as he heard the testimony of others concerning his involvement, which most likely rang true to him. Moments away from learning the jury's verdict on all 12 charges (including felony kidnapping, armed robbery, and conspiracy), O.J. could be seen loosening both his collar and his tie. No doubt he was literally feeling the heat in the second most decisive moment in his life. O.J. stood with a loosened tie while the guilty verdict was read, ironically 13 years to the day after he was acquitted of the double murder charges for his wife, Nicole, and her friend Ron Goldman.

The big gulp

Another telltale sign of deception is gulping or swallowing hard. This swallowing is the result of the autonomic nervous system kicking in. Because the Adam's apple (or *laryngeal prominence*) is often more visible in men, it is easier to see this in men. (You can see it in women—it's just not as obvious.) The liar will usually stop midsentence to swallow automatically. When a person is feeling anxious or doing or saying something he shouldn't, saliva production will often diminish. As a result, the throat will feel dry and scratchy. In order to lubricate the throat and continue speaking (read: lying), the liar swallows, which relieves that uncomfortable, tight, scratchy feeling.

Photo 7-19: Lance Armstrong gulped and swallowed hard during his Oprah interview when he watched video depositions of himself lying. Photo credit: Getty Images.

Lance Armstrong could often be seen gulping and swallowing hard throughout his interview with Oprah, particularly when he discussed his doping. It was most obvious when Lance was watching past videos of himself in deposition tapes as he blatantly lied about his drug use. As he watched himself on camera, you could clearly observe his Adam's apple bobbing up and down as he swallowed during those critical moments.

WHEN WORDS AND BODY LANGUAGE DON'T MATCH

The body usually doesn't lie. In fact, the limbic system deep in the recesses of our brain will often "out" us by betraying the truth and the true emotion that goes along with it. You may have noticed that when you agree with someone and you are telling the truth, your head will often automatically nod up and down, indicating that your body is essentially "agreeing" with what you are saying. Similarly, your head will often automatically shake back and forth when you truthfully deny something, which, again, is your body's way of supporting the veracity of what you're saying. When you lie, however, there is confusion within the brain. If you deny something when the real answer is yes, your body will often contradict the lie by automatically causing you to nod your head. Consequently, the truth leaks out unbidden. Unsurprisingly, this lack of congruence between what we say (or words) and our body language (whether we nod or shake our head) is often a huge "tell" of deception.

Several times during his interview with Oprah, Lance Armstrong exhibited this lack of congruence between what he was saying and how he moved his head. This inconsistency, particularly taken within the greater context of his typical speech patterns and body language, indicated that he was most likely not telling the absolute truth about everything, or, at the very least, that he was omitting critical information.

CHANGES IN THE HANDS AND ARMS

Finger and nail biting

When people are nervous or anxious, it is not uncommon to see them with their fingers in their mouth. Since lying can be a stressful event, they may bite their fingers or nails to help relieve the stress and tension.

Photo 7-20: Finger- or nail-biting is often a sign that someone is anxious—or lying. Photo Credit: Milkovsa/Shutterstock, Inc.

Covering the mouth

A telltale sign of lying is that a person will automatically put their hands over their mouth when they don't want to deal with an issue or answer a question. In the photo on page 102 a reporter is asking Lance Armstrong about his doping. Whatever his actual response was, his hand over his mouth spoke volumes. Upon hearing the question, Armstrong's hand almost immediately shot up over his mouth, as if to indicate he wasn't talking.

It is a primitive, instinctual response to place your hand over your mouth to shut yourself up. Children do this quite often, particularly when you tell them to be quiet. And both adults and children do this when they have done something wrong, like lying. It's an emblematic gesture that essentially says, *I will say no more.* Little Falcon Heene did this right after he spilled the beans on CNN that his family's story about his being carried away in a makeshift balloon was a hoax. After the press descended on the family's home in Colorado, and Falcon and his family went outside for the first time since the hoax was uncovered, Falcon immediately covered his

Photo 7-21: Lance Armstrong covering his mouth during a press conference after he is asked about his use of performance-enhancing drugs. Photo credit: Jennifer Lorenzini/Splash News.

mouth with both of his hands as if to indicate that he didn't want to say anything else—especially not to the press that was eagerly waiting outside.

When adults put their hands over their lips, it means they aren't revealing everything and they just don't want to tell the truth. They are literally closing off communication. This was clearly evident in Lance Armstrong's interview with Oprah Winfrey. Although he revealed a lot of information, his body language indicated that there was much he was still withholding.

It can also mean that the person has been caught in a lie and is embarrassed to say anything further. When Oprah called Lance to task on his egregious actions by stating, "You were suing people, yet you know they are telling the truth," we saw him slap his hand over his mouth, as seen in the previous photo. He knew he was busted and hence there was nothing more he could say.

Covering vulnerable body parts

Oftentimes when people have something to hide, they will place their hands over a vulnerable part of the body such as the throat, chest, abdomen, or private parts. John Edwards consistently covered his groin throughout his *Nightline* interview. Each time the subject of his paternity came up, he would strategically clasp his hands over his genitals. When people are feeling vulnerable or uneasy about being caught in a lie, it is not uncommon to see their hands positioned in this manner.

Other vulnerable areas that are often covered during deception are the abdomen and chest. When you see someone suddenly place his hands over his abdomen or hold on to his stomach, it may also be an indication of deception. The reason for this is, once again, the autonomic nervous system (over which we have no control) suddenly kicks in, which gets the digestive juices flowing overtime. It also causes the smooth muscles of the stomach and digestive tract to suddenly contract, which may give the sensation of pain or of having to move one's bowels.

Photo 7-22: Tiger Woods placing his arm over his chest and one hand over his throat, two very vulnerable areas of the body. Photo credit: Splash News.

If someone immediately places his hand over his heart or chest area, he may be feeling sudden muscle tension in this important area of the body so necessary to life. Shortly after the scandal of his multiple infidelities broke, Tiger Woods was apologetic and ostensibly attempting to repair his marriage. In many photos, he and his wife, Elin, could be seen walking together yet apart, with a great deal of physical distance between them. This likely echoed the emotional distance between them and the pain they were both experiencing. It seems understandable that Tiger would subconsciously cover one of his most vulnerable organs, his heart. It is heartening and perhaps too optimistic to think that he might have been broken-hearted, knowing the pain he caused his wife and the harm he caused to his own reputation. Also note in the photo that his hand is strategically placed over another vulnerable part of his body, his throat. When someone's hands remain fixed in position covering a vulnerable body part, chances are he has something to hide. Perhaps Tiger was hiding his true feelings of devastation—devastation that he had hurt Elin, and devastation over being hurt by the hostile reaction from both the public and his commercial endorsers.

When people lie it's not uncommon to see them put their hand over their throat/Adam's apple, another very vulnerable area of the body, and leave it there.

Arm crossing, torso shielding, and the cold shoulder

People cross their arms for the most benign reasons—perhaps they are cold, or they just feel more comfortable in that position. However, one arm crossed over another or one arm slung across one's torso can also mean something very different. The gesture can serve as a self-protective shield if the person is feeling insecure or vulnerable. When someone suddenly crosses his arms in the middle of a conversation, he may be showing you through his behavior that he's not telling you the truth or, at the very least, not revealing everything. What he has done is essentially block you from the truth by forming a physical barrier with his arms.

In an exclusive photo of Tiger Woods following his cheating scandal, he can be seen shielding his torso with one arm. The photo indicates that he was likely closed off to Elin; and indeed, their facial expressions show that they were experiencing a great deal of emotional pain. Perhaps the fact that Tiger was closed off to Elin, as demonstrated by his arm positioned over his torso, was the result of more and more women coming forward and claiming that they had had affairs with Tiger, as well.

You can often see celebrities make this gesture when they are being interviewed. When the questions get too personal or uncomfortable, their arms will usually "run interference" in front of their body.

Photo 7-23: American Idol judges with Nicki Minaj (far right) crossing her arms to keep Mariah blocked out, while Mariah gives Nicki the cold shoulder. Photo credit: Getty News Entertainment.

We also cross our arms when we don't like the person or people we're talking to. In Hollywood, actors are usually pretty conscious about not alienating anyone in the business or burning bridges needlessly. But the previous photo of the *American Idol* judges demonstrates that body language usually does not lie. There appears to be some truth in the media firestorm that erupted concerning a possible feud between the two singers. While they both insisted to the press that there were no hard feelings between them, their body language said something quite different.

Mariah had a lot to say with her body language, as well. In the photo you can see that she has literally given Nicki the cold shoulder. She has raised her shoulder in a subconscious attempt to block Nicki and create a physical barrier between them. So even though Mariah never publicly admitted having any bad feelings toward Nicki, her cold shoulder said it all, despite all the smiles and kind words.

Whenever I am asked to provide an analysis of the status of a couple's relationship, based solely on looking at their body language, whenever I see a cold shoulder—in which one raises his/her shoulder to block out the other—I know the relationship is in trouble. So if you are talking to someone and she suddenly raises her shoulder, particularly if you have just broached a critical or sensitive subject, there is a good possibility that she is lying to you; she is literally trying to close you off or block you out with her shoulder.

The "itchy scratchies"

When a liar's autonomic nervous system goes into overdrive, the increased blood flow and expanded capillaries often cause an itching sensation. This is why someone who is telling a lie may suddenly scratch the skin on his head, face, neck, or arms.

Here we see O.J. Simpson scratching his face after Catherine Crier asked him a probing question. This was yet another body language signal that may have indicated that Simpson was not being forthright in his answers.

In his interview with Oprah Winfrey, Lance Armstrong exhibited a major case of the "itchy scratchies" after Oprah asked him why he had sued the people who had accused him (truthfully) about his doping. He immediately got the "itchy scratchies" on his chin and lower jaw. His scratching reflected that he clearly knew that what he had done was very serious and very, very wrong. His body knew it was wrong, too. As soon as the topic was brought up, those changes in his blood flow (remember the autonomic nervous system?) created an itchy sensation on his chin, which he automatically scratched.

Photo 7-24: O.J. Simpson displaying a raging case of the "itchy scratchies" during a Court TV interview, 10 years after his wife's murder. Photo credit: AdLIB Design/Splash News.

Remember that scratching can occur whether the person is actually speaking a lie or just thinking about a lie they have already told. So whenever you suddenly see someone scratching, never rule out that there could be deception in the works.

Hand rubbing/wringing, tapping, grooming, and picking

When people are anxious about lying, you will often see them playing with their fingers, tapping their fingers on something, or picking at their fingers. It's the body's way of relieving anxiety.

Here we see Lindsay Lohan in one of her early court appearances in Beverly Hills, engaging in the stress-relieving, self-soothing, finger-picking behavior. You often see this when someone feels threatened or feels that her lie is about to be revealed. This was clearly the case with Lindsay. She was caught publicly lying on numerous occasions throughout the years; here, she was reacting to hearing an uncomfortable truth about herself in the courtroom.

Photo 7-25: Lindsay Lohan in a Beverly Hills courtroom fiddling with her fingers. Photo credit: Pool/London Entertainment/Splash News.

Likewise, when you see someone rubbing or wringing her hands, she may be comforting herself in order to help mitigate anxiety. With the changes in the autonomic nervous system, there may also be changes in body temperature. Thus, the body may suddenly become too hot or too cold. If it becomes too cold, the extremities, such as the hands, are usually the first to be affected. The automatic, natural response is to create friction and generate heat by rubbing the hands together. So if you ask someone a pointed question and he rubs his hands together, this could be a sign that he's not telling the truth.

Such self-soothing can also take the form of brushing imaginary lint off the body or playing with the hair.

Photo 7-26: Lindsay Lohan playing with her hair in court as she listens to the allegations against her. Photo credit: Pool/London Entertainment/ Splash News.

Here we see Lindsay Lohan displaying more self-soothing behavior, as she plays with her hair before she is sentenced to jail. Liars will often fiddle with their hair as a means of comforting themselves. The behavior can also reflect indecisiveness and insecurity concerning how best to spin their lies.

Several years ago, the Heene family caused a national scandal when they duped the world into believing that their 6-year-old son, Falcon, was caught in a homemade Mylar balloon that had come untethered. After they "miraculously" found Falcon hiding in their attic, they went on national TV to tell their story. Little Falcon, the center of this tale, ended up leaking out the truth about what had really happened. He admitted to CNN's Wolf Blitzer that they "did [it] for TV." His father got defensive as he hemmed and hawed, trying to backpedal and repair what Falcon had accidently revealed.

Richard's wife, Mayumi's body language was also revealing. Before Falcon blurted out the truth, Wolf Blitzer asked Mayumi to describe what had happened. As Mayumi told the story, she constantly kept brushing her thighs with her hands as though she were grooming herself. She did this the entire time she was being interviewed. Mayumi knew this was a hoax and she knew she was lying; her way of dealing with the discomfort was to subconsciously brush the lie away, as evidenced in the emblematic grooming gesture. Allegedly in exchange for not being deported to Japan and losing her family, she later admitted to law enforcement that she had lied. So when you see someone repeatedly groom herself—brush or pick imaginary lint off of her person, play with her hair, or pick at her fingers—chances are, she's lying.

Palms toward the body

During deception, a person's palm or palms will often be turned away from you so that you can only see the backs of the hands. Conversely, if someone is telling the truth, you will usually see both palms exposed in an open position, indicating that the person has nothing to hide.

Photo 7-27: Lance Armstrong gestures with his palms toward his body during his interview with Oprah, a possible signal of deception. Photo credit: Getty News Entertainment.

When cyclist Lance Armstrong went on *Oprah* in an attempt to explain himself, he frequently made deceptive gestures with his palms facing his body. When people gesture toward their body in this way, they are being guarded and self-protective, and likely have something to hide. Contrast this with someone gesturing away from his body, with palms facing out; this is the body language of openness and forthrightness. While Armstrong appeared to be truthful throughout much of the interview, this photo indicates that this was *not* one of those times.

People often mix the truth in with their lies; they may even be lying to themselves. In that case, we often see a conflicting double gesture (lying/not lying), as we see in the photo of Lindsay Lohan pleading with the judge to not give her jail time. The palm of one of her hands is up, showing truthfulness, while the other palm is facing down, exposing the back of her hand, showing deceitfulness. The conflicting gestures also indicate that she was likely not being 100-percent honest with herself, either, in terms of how responsible she felt for getting herself into that predicament in the first place.

Photo 7-28: Lindsay Lohan in a Beverly Hills courtroom exhibiting both deceptive and non-deceptive gestures.
Photo credit: Pool/London Entertainment/Splash News.

Finger pointing—the body language of righteous indignation

One of the most famous lies of the previous century was told when President Clinton stood up in front of the American people and told the lie that was heard around the world: "I never had sex with that woman—Ms. Lewinsky." That lie and his cheating not only strained his marriage and destroyed his credibility, but it almost cost him the presidency.

Photo 7-29: President Bill Clinton pointing at the American public as he angrily denied the allegations against him. Photo credit: Joyce Naltchayan/Staff AP/Getty Images.

This historical picture of President Clinton angrily pointing his index finger, admonishing the American people for not believing that he didn't have an affair with a White House intern, will be forever etched into everyone's mind. Finger-pointing can be a very hostile and angry gesture, certainly not something one would expect in a public speech by a sitting president. Clinton's overreaction and defensiveness was almost certainly due to his guilt for lying to the public and his family; he had indeed had sexual relations with "that woman—Ms. Lewinsky."

When a liar becomes hostile or defensive, he is attempting to turn the tables on you. He is making you wrong for even thinking a person as "righteous" and "honorable" as he is could do such a thing as a lie. Now the focus is on you and your lack of trust, not his lie. This is righteous indignation. The finger-pointing is a subconscious way of admonishing or threatening you into believing him; it's a kind of nonverbal "punctuation" that emphasizes his wish—no, demand—to be believed.

Photo 7-30: O.J. Simpson pointing his finger during a Court TV interview, emphasizing his righteous indignation and his wish to be believed. Photo credit: AdLIB Design/Splash News.

O.J. Simpson revealed his desperation to be believed not only by leaning forward throughout his interview, but also by his hostile finger-pointing.

Hiding the hands and arms

When people are engaged in deception, they often hide their hands. They either place their hands in their pockets, behind them, or under something (a table, for example). They also may cup their hands in a subconscious attempt to make their hands smaller. Keep in mind that people often put their hands in their pockets just because it's comfortable; as always, context is key in deciphering deception. However, if, during the course of your conversation with someone, she suddenly thrusts her hands into her pockets, chances are you've hit on something that she doesn't want to share with you. Again, this is an emblematic, self-protective gesture; she is hiding her hands, just as she is hiding the truth.

When actors Brad Pitt and Angelina Jolie were promoting their film *Mr. and Mrs. Smith*, there was rampant speculation that they were having an affair. This turned out to be true, even though Brad Pitt was still married to actress Jennifer Aniston at the time. Brad and Angelina—"Brangelina," as they are known in the tabloids—made every attempt to hide their romance and play it cool in front of the public, but their body language spoke volumes.

Photo 7-31: Brad Pitt and Angelina Jolie at a press junket for their film *Mr. and Mrs. Smith*. Photo credit: Russ Einhorn/ Splash News.

One of the most telling signs they were lying was the fact that Brad's hands were constantly in his pockets. It showed that he had something to hide. Angelina always had one or both of her hands hidden behind her, as well. They were hiding their hands and arms as a subconscious way of hiding their feelings toward one another so that the public wouldn't figure out what was *really* going on. But it wasn't working.

They also did their best to keep a significant physical distance between them at all times, as you can see in the previous photo. They even kept their gazes fixed in front of them and refused to look at one another. But that wasn't working, either. If you really look closely at the photo, you can see that their bodies were like two magnets gravitating toward each other. Of course, their efforts to appear separate made the public question their relationship even more, since most costars are usually seen hugging and touching one another, or at least standing next to one another in camaraderie when promoting a film.

But the main giveaway that something was going on between them could be seen in the position of their feet. When people like one another, their feet will actually gravitate toward each other. As you can see in the photo, Brad's right foot was inching toward Angelina, and her left foot was subtly inching toward Brad.

When someone has something to hide, as Kris Humphries did, they often tend to hide their fingers or their entire hands. On the next page we see Kris Humphries with his fingers jammed in his pocket instead of lovingly holding hands with his new wife, Kim.

Photo 7-32: Kris Humphries hiding his fingers
in his pocket as he hides the status of his ill-fated marriage
to Kim Kardashian. Photo credit: VLUV/Splash News.

Cupping the hands or making a fist

Liars will also sometimes cup their hands or make a slight fist. A fist most often reflects anger or at least tension, so when someone suddenly cups his hands or makes an actual fist, pay attention to the content of the conversation and what could be triggering these kinds of feelings. In many interviews we can see Lance Armstrong cupping his fingers into a rounded position as he is questioned about his doping. He did exactly this during an interview in Austin, Texas, in 2006, and during a CNN interview with Larry King. The cupped hand indicated his anger at the interviewers for doubting and questioning him. In essence, the truth hit too close to home, because, in his heart of hearts, he knew he was lying about taking performance-enhancing drugs to win races.

THE AGONY OF THE FEET

Believe it or not, you can sometimes tell whether someone is lying just by looking at her feet. Someone may be sitting perfectly still, but if she shuffles her feet at a critical juncture in the conversation, she may not be telling you the full truth at that moment.

Photo 7-33: Whether the person is standing or sitting, if the heel is off the ground, it can be a sign of deception.
Photo credit: O. Guuero/Shutterstock, Inc.

When someone lifts her heel off the ground as she's speaking to you, as illustrated in this photo, it could be a sign of the "flight" part of the "fight of flight" response, which makes the liar want to flee the scene of the crime, as it were. This can also be the case if someone's feet are suddenly pointed toward the door or an exit.

When you see someone sitting or standing with both sets of toes pointed inward (the pigeon-toed stance), it can mean that the person is being guarded and self-protective, and possibly dishonest. It can also be a sign of a hidden agenda.

Before Katie Holmes suddenly and secretively left Tom Cruise, she remained guarded about her feelings for him for a variety of reasons. According to the press, she had concerns about her daughter being raised as a Scientologist. In this photo you can see this self-protectiveness in the position of her toes pointing toward one another. Tom's feet tell a completely different story, however. His right foot is pointed directly at Katie, which indicates how much he likes her. Their contrasting feet positions clearly reveal that their feelings for one another were not mutual at the time this photo was taken. Had Tom been aware of the meaning of Katie's body language, perhaps he wouldn't have been as shocked as people said he was when Katie secretly moved out of his home, fled to the East Coast, and filed for divorce not six months after this photo was taken.

Photo 7-34: Katie Holmes and Tom Cruise at the premiere of *Ghost Protocol*. Katie's body language may be showing signals of self-protection and deception. Photo courtesy of Lakota/ Splash News.

This pigeon-toed stance is often seen in young children who have done something wrong and are lying about it. So, parents beware!

Photo 8-1: Lance Armstrong avoiding eye contact with Oprah during his interview.Photo Credit: Getty Entertainment News.

During his interview with Oprah, Lance Armstrong had a hard time looking at his interviewer. This was particularly evident during the specific times he was likely still engaged in deception.

Liars who constantly break eye contact are uncomfortable with intimacy, at least at that moment; they would rather control or manipulate you through their lies. If they look directly at you they might feel intimidated and/or incapable of maintaining the upper hand, their "power over" you. They may also not want to look at you looking at them lying. Such liars will look to the right, to the left, up, or down; it doesn't matter. Personally I find no significance in the direction of the eye movement, only in the fact that they have broken eye contact.

Embarrassment is another reason liars avoid eye contact. Notre Dame football star Manti Te'o couldn't look at the ESPN reporter who was interviewing him about his fictitious girlfriend. He both closed *and* covered his eyes, as he literally didn't want to see the mess he had created. When he insisted, "I know it sounds crazy, but I am innocent," Manti was still lying. He knew he wasn't "innocent" because at that point he was still being dishonest. He was continuing to lie about "Lennay's" death and her funeral even though he was already aware that he had been catfished.

Photo 8-2: Bernard Madoff refused to look any of his victims in the eye when he gave his cursory and insincere courtroom apology. Photo credit: Splash News.

Disgraced financier Bernard Madoff did not look at any of the three investors who spoke at his sentencing hearing, even when one of the three turned in Madoff's direction and tried to address him directly. When Madoff finally turned to the investors and gave a brief and insincere apology, still he refused to look at them. In my opinion, the reason for his lack of eye contact was due to his shame and embarrassment over getting caught and losing his sense of power over others. His apologetic words were empty because he never visually connected with those he had hurt. This was his opportunity to engage with and even make some amends to those whose finances he had recklessly ruined. The fact that he refused to look at them told them that he didn't really care about them; even then, it was all about him.

Unless you are dealing with someone who truly doesn't know right from wrong, a liar knows when he/she is about to tell a lie. That is why liars often look down in order to focus on the tale they are about to spin or have already spun. After Tiger Woods was caught cheating on his wife with numerous women, he constantly looked down during his speech at a press conference. It made many people question his sincerity. It made them wonder whether he was apologizing only as an attempt to repair his reputation and keep himself from losing future endorsements. His lack of eye contact reeked of insincerity to many (if not most) who watched him that day. That, in addition to pursed lips, spoke volumes about his willingness to admit his unfaithfulness to the world. It indicated he may have even been forced into doing the press conference by his handlers.

Oftentimes people who are lying will look down because they do not want to be distracted by the negative reactions of others. Perhaps this was another reason why Bernard Madoff continued to look down as he rattled off his empty apology. This downward gaze also helps the liar more easily concentrate on his mission to deceive, as it did for John Edwards during his *Nightline* interview. Edwards simply could not look Bob Woodruff in the eye as he, Edwards, lied about not being his baby's biological father (which, of course, he was forced to admit months later).

A liar may also actually cover his eyes with his hands to avoid seeing and being seen. Because it can be very tiring to lie and keep all the facts straight, a liar will often cover or press on his eyes in order to relieve the muscular tension and fatigue in this area. The autonomic nervous system can trigger the muscles of the body to work overtime, which includes the tiny muscles around the eyes.

Photo 8-3: Covering the eyes or pressing on the eyes with the hands can be a form of self-soothing during moments of deception. Photo credit: Robert Kneschke/Shutterstock, Inc.

Staring

Of course, the converse can also hold true: an uncomfortable, protracted, unblinking stare, with eyes wide open, can indicate deception, as well. This is often the liar's attempt to look someone in the eye so that it will appear as though she/he is being totally honest. It's a form of overcompensation.

Apparently no one was better at making steady, staring eye contact than financial scammer Bernard Madoff. How else could he have seduced some of the nation's most powerful investors? Even the richest, the most famous and powerful people fell for his scheme. Had they known to be wary of those who stare and constantly maintain eye contact, they may have had the sense to avoid doing business with Madoff. But unfortunately, most were charmed or hypnotized by his stare, as they misinterpreted it as genuine caring about them and their financial future.

In this rare photo of Madoff, taken before he was caught, you can get a better idea of how he was able to seduce potential investors by his stare. Madoff was known for always looking people in the eye and making them feel good about themselves. As Diana Henriques, a reporter who recently interviewed him behind bars, said, "He never took his eyes off of me. He leaned forward and was very interested in everything I had to say" (from her *New York Times* article, "The Wizard of Lies: Bernie Madoff"). Henriques's statement clearly shows how Madoff was and obviously still is a good listener. He knew the power of a constant eye contact to make people think he cared when, in reality, he couldn't have cared less.

Photo 8-4: Disgraced financier Bernard Madoff was known to stare directly into clients' and prospective clients' eyes, likely to control and manipulate.
Photo credit: Excusive Candid/Splash News.

Madoff, like most con men, overcompensated and stared at people longer than usual, often without blinking at regular intervals. The smiles of such con men are typically fake, as well. If you cover Madoff's lower face in the previous photo, you will see that his mouth is smiling but his eyes are not. This half smile reveals the con's ambivalence toward his victims. He is trying hard to be pleasant, ingratiating, and likeable, but his cold, level gaze indicates that he knows exactly what he is doing.

When people tell the truth, most will occasionally shift their eyes around and may even look away from time to time. Liars, on the other hand, will use a cold, steady gaze to intimidate and control, as convicted murderer Drew Peterson did. He did this during interviews to make people think he was likeable, honest, and, above all, innocent, which of course it didn't. In fact, while he was in the makeup room at a major cable network, the makeup artist told me personally that she felt he was hitting on her. She said that Peterson "wouldn't stop staring" at her as he looked directly into her eyes, refusing to break eye contact.

My personal thoughts were that his staring at her was not seductive at all, but instead his way of intimidating this unconventional-looking, tattooed, pierced, very slight woman. I believe this was Peterson's attempt to exert power and control over someone he didn't understand, an unknown quantity, as it were. He may have done the same thing when he was a police officer, staring to intimidate and control those he arrested, not to mention his many wives, over whom he clearly exerted a great deal of control.

People will sometimes stare like this when they feel defensive. Making the other person look away or blink first means they have succeeded in intimidating that person; they have the upper hand. No doubt this is what Lance Armstrong was trying to do when he stared down an interviewer who questioned him about his alleged doping. This arrogant gesture was congruent with his other behaviors—particularly, suing for defamation those who questioned or reported him, when he knew all along that they were telling the truth.

Photo 8-5: Lance Armstrong staring at someone who questioned his use of performance-enhancing drugs. His stare was almost certainly meant to intimidate. Photo credit: Jennifer Lorenzini/Splash News.

Glaring

Glaring is a lot different than staring because it occurs in a flash of anger, as opposed to a steady and more consistent gaze. But it is still a gaze of hostility. It is a narrow-eyed look or glance that only lasts a short period of time. It is a form of ocular punctuation that says, *I am looking at you to make sure you are showing signs that you believe the lie I have just told you—you had better believe me.* Glaring also says, *I am angry that my lie is being questioned.*

In this photo, we see a finger-pointing Clinton's angry glare as he insists that he is innocent and didn't have sexual relations with Ms. Lewinsky. If you see a glare like this, know that the person is either angry or lying—or both.

Photo 8-6: President Bill Clinton glaring icily as he denies having sexual relations with Monica Lewinsky. Photo credit: Joyce Naltchayan/Staff AP/Getty Images.

The wide eyes of surprise

When people are engaged in deception you will often see their eyes widen and their eyebrows and forehead rise in a look of surprise or shock. It's a subconscious facial expression of "duped delight" wherein the liar is thrilled he got away with his deceit and is actually taking pleasure in reaping the benefits of the lie. Deep down a liar is usually surprised when he gets away with a lie; he finds it incredible that he hasn't been caught. Hence the wide-eyed look of surprise that surfaced periodically on Lance Armstrong's face prior to and during the scandal. The fact that he was able to get away with winning the Tour de France by cheating so many times was clearly surprising even to him.

The wide eyes of surprise often shows up when (a) something has compromised the liar's lie, (b) the liar gets a sense that someone has figured her out, or (c) when the liar is directly confronted with her lie—in other words, when she has been busted. This expression often shows up at the exact moment the liar realizes that no one is believing her lies. When this happens, the whites of the eyes become much more visible and the eyes appear large and saucer-like. In Lindsay Lohan's case, this happened when she heard a convincing statement in the courtroom that may have exposed her deception.

Photo 8-7: Lindsay Lohan showing the wide eyes of surprise as she listens to true testimony about herself and appears surprised or stunned by it. Photo credit: Pool/London Entertainment/Splash News.

Larry King is usually a benign and supportive interviewer, but when he directly and rather boldly confronted Lance Armstrong about his drug use, Lance's eyes got visibly larger, showing more and more *sclera* (the "whites" of the eyes), as he attempted to explain himself.

There is perhaps no better example of this phenomenon than in this photo of O.J. Simpson, as he muses aloud about what he would do if his children (then 18 and 15) ever asked what happened to their mother. The interviewer, Catherine Crier, and indeed most people who watched the interview, found it incredible that his children never asked about or discussed their mother up to that point.

Photo 8-8: O.J. Simpson displaying the wide eyes of surprise. The whites of his eyes are clearly visible here as he appears to manufacture a story during a Court TV interview. Photo credit: AdLIB Design/Splash News.

Rapid eye blinking

One of the most common "tells" that someone is lying is rapid and unusual eye blinking. This is often an automatic reaction and a strong indication of stress and fear—in this case, the fear of being found out. Perhaps the most widely known study of blinking and its relation to thought processes was undertaken by those who analyzed former President Richard Nixon's infamous "I am not a crook" speech, during certain parts of which he blinked abnormally rapidly. This indicated to researchers that he was not telling the truth at those times.

There are countless other examples of politicians from all political parties and all walks of life who have been observed blinking their eyes rapidly as they lied to their constituents. During his *Nightline* interview with reporter Bob Woodruff, John Edwards blinked his eyes in rapid succession whenever he was confronted with a question that he didn't want to answer. When he finally did answer, he often lied outright while blinking rapidly. He almost seemed to have a tic when he insisted that it was "physically impossible" for him to be the father of his mistress, Rielle Hunter's baby.

Eye rubbing

Lying takes a lot of effort. It's tiring to have to always remain on your toes in order to maintain the lie. When we are tired we will often rub our eyes, just as children do. When a suspect is being interrogated after continually lying to authorities you can sometimes observe this behavior. Eye rubbing is a pretty common occurrence in the courtroom, as well. It is a sudden automatic reaction to try and soothe and release the tension and fatigue in the muscles around the eyes.

Eye rubbing may also be a part of the "itchy scratchies" that occur when the blood flow increases and small capillaries expand around the eyes. It's part of that same autonomic response that kicks in when there is pressure, stress, or tension. Children commonly rub their eyes when they are overtired and they are lying. Whether child or adult, if someone covers his eyes with his hand(s) as he rubs them, it may indicate that he is hiding figuratively, as well—a clear signal of deception.

Shifty eyes

Liars often look to the side when they lie. They may look to the right or to the left, or they may shift their eyes back and forth as though they were searching for an answer. This shifty-eyed look was evident as former President Richard Nixon gave his infamous "I am not a crook" speech. Nixon's eyes shifted to the right as he stated, "In all my years of public life I have never obstructed justice." Nixon obviously knew that he had indeed obstructed justice, to the extent that he was eventually impeached for the Watergate incident.

When we lie about how we really feel about someone, we often shift our eyes in order to view a person from the side. For example, while Nicki Minaj keeps her head positioned straight ahead, her eyes shift to the right as she peers at Mariah Carey. Mariah, on the other hand, is more upfront about her gaze and moves her head to glance at Nicki.

Photo 8-9: Nicki Minaj (far right) looking askance at fellow judge Mariah Carey (far left). Photo credit: Getty News Entertainment.

In my opinion, Nicki's sidelong glare confirms that there was no love lost between her and her fellow *American Idol* judge Mariah Carey. Even though both publically claimed that there was no tension or friction between them, their facial language "tells" revealed a much different story.

Squinting

When people are angry or in a state of disbelief/suspicion, you will often see them narrow their gaze disapprovingly. Liars will often squint in a display of righteous indignation, as well. They look at others disapprovingly for having the audacity to question them or doubt the veracity of what they are saying. If a liar squints as he is lying, it is usually involuntary.

In essence he is subconsciously evaluating himself in terms of the negative words that have just come out of his mouth. His squinting essentially says, *I don't want you to detect my deception.*

Photo 8-10: O.J. Simpson squints during his Court TV interview 10 years after the murder of his wife. Photo credit: AdLIB Design/Splash News.

Squinting can also indicate that the liar is trying to emphasize a particular point. In this case it is an expression of self-righteous indignation. Clearly O.J. Simpson has consistently shown righteous indignation throughout the years every time he's been questioned about his involvement in his wife's murder. In this photo his squinting likely reflects his annoyance at being asked so many questions, which, ironically, has caused many people to believe that he may have had some involvement in her death.

Lance Armstrong squinted his way through many of his interviews, too, particularly when he's had to field serious questions pertaining to his use of performance-enhancing drugs. His squinting probably reflected his anger and discomfort over having to answer these questions. Similarly, we saw former President Clinton squinting as he indignantly lied, "I did not have an affair...." His squinting reflected his anger that the public would have the audacity to even entertain the thought of him doing something so egregious.

Raised eyebrows and wrinkled forehead

Similar to the "eyes of surprise," raised eyebrows and/or wrinkled forehead can also indicate deception. As you will see in the following photo of O.J. Simpson, he exhibits this facial language as he discussed his wife's murder 10 years after the fact. These signals were especially evident after the interviewer asked him some pointed and probing questions pertaining to the murder of his wife and her friend.

Photo 8-11: O. J. Simpson with raised eyebrows and wrinkled forehead, two common signals of deception, during his *Court TV* interview. Photo credit: AdLIB Design/Splash News.

Researchers at the University of British Columbia found that liars are often betrayed by these small muscle movements, most likely due to tension and the resulting reaction of the autonomic nervous system. We saw a great deal of this facial language during the many interviews that Lance Armstrong gave throughout the years, when he was repeatedly asked questions pertaining to his doping. His expression indicated surprise and indignation that anyone would dare question his integrity.

THE NOSE KNOWS

When the autonomic nervous system takes over, the expanding capillaries often cause the mucous membranes to expand, as well, which often creates swelling and an itching sensation in the nose. Believe it or not, a liar's nose will actually grow, just like the fictional Disney character Pinocchio, only to a much smaller degree. That is why it is not uncommon to see liars pull at or scratch their nose as they lie. This behavior often occurs in children. They will often do this when they hear others telling lies, too—for example, their parents and siblings.

"Balloon dad" Richard Heene lied to the press about the hoax he had created, and so did his older son, Bradford. Bradford clearly knew his father had been lying throughout all of the interviews about his younger son, Falcon, and about his involvement in the hoax. That is why Bradford was often seen scratching his nose during interviews and photo opportunities.

Celebrities will often scratch their noses when they are being interviewed but don't want to reveal everything about their personal relationships.

Photo 8-12: Jennifer Aniston scratching her nose on the set of the *Early Show* on CBS. Photo credit: James Devaney/Splash News.

Ever since her marriage to Brad Pitt ended in such a scandalous way, with his leaving her for his *Mr. and Mrs. Smith* costar, Angelina Jolie, it seems that Jennifer Aniston's love life has been a hot topic. Reporters constantly want to know whom she is dating, whether she's engaged, or if she's pregnant. Like most people, Jennifer no doubt prefers to keep some things private. Her scratching may have indicated a lie by omission—perhaps she wasn't sharing everything with her interviewer that day.

Sneezing

While sneezing may simply be due to allergies, a cold, or environmental irritants, it may also be a sign that someone's lying. Because the capillaries and blood vessels in the nose and in the mucus membranes tend to expand due to the actions of the autonomic nervous system, it is not uncommon to hear a sneeze as someone tells a lie. So the old superstition that we only "sneeze on the truth" is nothing more than a myth and an old wives' tale. In fact, it may very well be the opposite: that we "sneeze on a lie."

Children sneeze when they lie more often than adults. This is because children's nasal passages and mucus membranes are much more sensitive to those changes in the autonomic nervous system.

Flared nostrils

When people lie it is not uncommon to see the sides of their nose (the *alae*) flare slightly as they inhale. This is because they will often get short of breath, so they need to take in more air, more frequently. When the liar's autonomic nervous system kicks in and his/her body is working overtime, there is a dire need for more oxygen; this is evidenced in his/her inhaling more air through the nose.

Periodically throughout his *Oprah* interview, Lance Armstrong could be seen doing this kind nasal breathing, with the sides of his nose flared out. This may have been an indication that he was not being honest or withholding information during these moments.

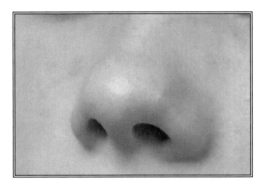

Photo 8-13: When the sides of nose (alae) flare out, it may be a signal of deception. Photo credit: Gleb Smenjuk/Shutterstock, Inc.

CHANGES IN THE MOUTH

Cotton mouth and lip licking

If you ever watch the videotaped interrogation of a suspect who is guilty, you will often observe that it becomes more and more difficult for her to speak. This is because her mouth has suddenly become very dry. When this happens, it literally feels as though there is cotton stuck to the roof of one's mouth. Law enforcement officers and interrogators call this *cotton mouth.* This occurs because the autonomic nervous system decreases salivary flow during times of stress, which of course dries out the mucous membranes of the mouth. When suspects who are suffering from cotton mouth are offered a glass of water, it is not uncommon to see them gulp down the entire thing at once to quench their thirst. This is further evidence that they were experiencing cotton mouth as they tried not to implicate themselves during the interrogation.

Another visual indication of cotton mouth is the presence of dried mucus or white spittle on the corners of the lips on both sides of a person's mouth, on the lower lip, and even on the sides of the tongue. On the day of his sentencing for armed robbery and kidnapping, O.J. Simpson could be seen licking the sides of his lips; clearly he was experiencing a case of cotton mouth as he waited to hear his fate, which was to essentially spend the rest of his life behind bars.

139

Photo 8-14: O.J. showing signs of cotton mouth during his Court TV interview. Photo credit: AdLIB Designs/Splash News.

Cotton mouth makes it difficult to move and manipulate the tongue around the lips and teeth, which makes it very difficult to speak. Because of the dried-out mucus membranes, the tongue seems to stick to the inner cheeks and roof of the mouth, thereby making the tongue feel and even appear thicker and wider.

In this photo of O.J. we see him wiping away the dried spittle that has accumulated in the corners of his mouth. This, too, is a sign of cotton mouth and dried-out mucus membranes, most likely due to deceptive behavior. Liars will often lick their lips in an attempt to alleviate the dryness, as well. Therefore, when you see someone licking his/her lips like this, it may be a signal of deception—depending, of course, on the person's baseline and the context.

The fake smile

In order for a smile to be genuine, four things must be present: one, the eyes should crinkle (with "crow's feet"); two, the apples of the cheeks should be raised; three, the teeth must be showing; and four, the lips should be parted and slanting upward. Unless you see all four of these signs, the person's smile is either phony, tense, or forced. She is trying to mask her true feelings.

Photo 8-15: Lance Armstrong's fake, tight-lipped grin as he is interviewed by a journalist at a press conference. Photo credit: Jennifer Lorenzini/Splash News.

Here we see Lance Armstrong being interviewed by a journalist and smiling a tense, fake smile as he is asked about the doping allegations against him. You could see a similar expression in a photo of him at the 2010 Tour de France ceremonies in France. His name has just been called to receive the award. He knows he is supposed to be happy, so he smiles, but the smile is not a genuine one. The apples of his cheeks are not raised, his eyes don't crinkle, and his lips are tightly pursed in a horizontal position, instead of slanting upward with his lips open and teeth showing. This very tense and fake smile likely reflected his true inner feelings—namely, that he could not be truly happy or elated about his achievements when he knew that he cheated, not only in that particular race, but in all of his previous Tour de France races.

If you watch a rerun of the *Nightline* interview of John Edwards, it is laden with examples of his fake smile, in which his mouth is smiling but his eyes and cheeks are not. This phony smile is particularly evident as he denies paternity of Rielle Hunter's child and asserts, "I'll be happy to prove the child is not mine." He knew he was lying when he uttered those words because he knew all along that he was indeed the child's biological father.

Edwards even put this fake smile to work in his mug shot, as he attempted to give the impression that he was happy and all was well. The reality, of course, was that he was *not* at all happy about being arrested and forced to have his mug shot taken. No one could be genuinely happy about that! His eyes are not smiling, and there is marked tension in his lower jaw as his teeth appear to be clenched together, which does not happen in a genuine smile. In addition, the apples of his cheeks seem to droop downward as opposed to tilting upward, as they would in a real smile.

Photo 8-16: John Edwards's fake smile in his mug shot after being arrested for campaign finance fraud. Photo credit: Splash News.

In general, when someone is genuinely smiling, he or she will look directly at you, not down or to the side. Otherwise the smile is likely not genuine. During his *Nightline* interview, when Edwards lied about the paternity of his mistress's child, he often looked down as he grinned tensely. Even before the interview began, Edwards exhibited the same phony, tense smile that he put on for his mug shot. He continued with this fake display of happiness as he endeavored to flatter and ingratiate himself to the host of the show. While Edwards expressed how pleased he was to do the interview in order to be able to tell "his side of the story," his facial language indicated that he was in no way pleased. No one displaying a tense half-smile is pleased to do anything. These were all clear indications of deception.

Bernard Madoff was another liar who was adept at wielding a fake smile. Note his tight-lipped smile and unfriendly eyes as he left a court proceeding in 2008. This may have been an indication of nerves on his part. He wanted to appear cordial and friendly in an atmosphere where the press was shouting hostile words at him and the photographers were pushing him. In fact, one photographer actually came out from behind his camera to shove Madoff, to which Madoff responded angrily and admonished the photographer that there would be no pushing.

Photo 8-17: Bernard Madoff's phony smile so angered a photographer that he pushed Madoff. Photo credit: Splash News.

There was absolutely no reason why disgraced Penn State coach and convicted pedophile Jerry Sandusky would be smiling after he was found guilty on so many counts of child molestation. There was also no reason for him to be smiling after he was denied a new trial during a post-sentence motion. And there was definitely no reason for him to smile when he found out that he will be spending the rest of his life in prison (and likely fighting for his life when other prisoners inevitably attack him for being a pedophile).

If you look closely at his smile, however, it is a phony one. His teeth are clenched together and his eyes and the apple of his cheeks droop downward. That means that even though he was trying to smile on the outside, there was turmoil on the inside. Sandusky used his smile to not only charm his colleagues at Penn State, but also the players, the backers of his charity, the media, and even the children he victimized. Perhaps he was smiling in a subconscious effort to charm those who watched him walk by, so that they wouldn't think of him as the monster he really was.

The lip swing

When someone swings his lips to the side, or bites the inside of his lower lip as his swings it to the side, it is often a signal of deception.

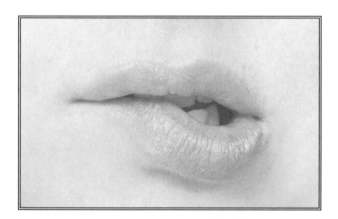

Photo 8-18: Swinging the lips to the side is often indicative of deception. Photo credit: Vladyslav Starozhylov/Shutterstock, Inc.

This "lip swing" is commonly seen when people are being deceptive about their feelings toward others. For instance, if someone really doesn't like you deep down, she will often "leak" these feelings out by swinging her lips to the side. Usually this involves just the lower lip, but sometimes it will involve only the upper lip. In that case it is called the "lip of disgust."

Photo 8-19: The lip of disgust often indicates deception.
Photo credit: Guryanov Andrey/Shutterstock, Inc.

You can often see this facial expression in couples who are having problems but trying to put on a happy face in front of friends and family. By the end of the evening you will sometimes see this lip of disgust sneak out, an expression of derision that tells you that their marriage is not so great after all, no matter how politely they may speak to one another. It can also often be spotted among competitive coworkers, employers, and employees. When someone harbors deep negative feelings toward you, but can't let those feelings out for fear of repercussions or upsetting a working relationship, this expression will usually surface eventually.

I once attending a course to become a mediator that was being taught by multiple professors. I noticed Professor X display the upper lip swing, the lip of disgust, as she was being introduced by Professor Y. Like clockwork, as she began her lecture moments later, she managed to get in a few "zings" about Professor Y and in fact continued insulting him throughout her lecture. It was clear that she couldn't stand Professor Y, and was basically forcing herself to be nice and civil to him. But even before she insulted him publically, her "lip of disgust" belied her true feelings.

Whether it involves the upper or lower lip, a lip swing clearly shows deception. John Edwards could be seen making this expression several times during his *Nightline* interview. He swung both his lips to the side while stating that his wife, Elizabeth, forgave him after learning of his affair. Edward's lip swing was a clear signal of deception. It subsequently came out in the press that Elizabeth had not forgiven him immediately upon learning of his affair and illegitimate child; instead, she allegedly kicked him out of the house. Edwards also showed this lip swing as he left the courtroom during his campaign finance fraud trial, which almost cost him his freedom. He tried to exude a happy-go-lucky appearance with a smile and pleasant banter; however, his lip swing showed that he was lying. It revealed that there was really nothing that he was happy about as he awaited his fate, which could very well have included prison time.

We consistently saw this lip swing with Susan Smith, the woman who claimed that her children had been taken by a "Black stranger," when in fact she was one who drove them into a river and killed them. Her lip swing, along with her fake tears, was clearly evident as she pleaded for the return of her children when she knew full well that she killed them. This same expression was also evident throughout her trial. When someone feels guilt, you will often see this telltale lip swing, a signal of deception in full force.

"Duping delight"—the subtle, fleeting, inappropriate smile

When someone suddenly smiles when he should be sad, serious, or upset, it is called "duping delight." This person is revealing that he is really happy, even if that happiness is inappropriate for the context. Perhaps the most disturbing example of a celebrity "duping delight" was seen in a *60 Minutes* interview of Arnold Schwarzenegger discussing his history of cheating on wife, Maria Shriver, and the resulting illegitimate son he created with their housekeeper.

In the interview, reporter Leslie Stahl directly confronts Arnold by saying, "In your book, you write that you had an affair with an actress in that movie. You cheated on Maria." Instead of looking contrite or having a serious facial expression, Arnold nods his head while leaking out a smug little smile. That smile indicates that he most likely had no remorse about cheating on Maria. Even though he remarked that he felt bad about what he did, his facial language revealed the complete opposite. In fact, as he recalled the affair with the actress in his mind, he appeared to actually feel good about it.

Terrorists who are captured often exhibit "duping delight." They may claim they have remorse for what they did, but inevitably a smile will leak out, just as it did with "Bali bomber" Huda bin Abdul Haq, also known as "Muklas." This man can be seen smiling in almost every photo. When a journalist asked him if he felt badly about what he had done, he said he felt bad that Muslims had died that day, but he was smiling as he said it. Perhaps this was a case of "duping delight," wherein he was secretly pleased that so many had died. *After all,* he may have thought, *what were Muslims doing at or near a bar in Bali?*

Pursed lips

When people purse their lips after they've told a lie, it usually means that they don't want to say anymore. Like a hand clapped over the mouth, it serves as a form of punctuation that says, *I've said my lie and now I'm done. I have nothing more to say!* After President Clinton told the lie that was heard around the world, he turned away from the audience and the cameras while keeping his lips tightly pursed. This expression communicated wordlessly that he had nothing more to say to the public about the matter. Interestingly, after he was acquitted of perjury and obstruction of justice, Clinton continued to purse his lips as he declared that he was "profoundly sorry...for what [he] said and did."

People sometimes purse their lips or press them together when they hear an unpleasant truth about themselves. They try to proclaim their innocence by sticking to their lie and remaining silent. It is their subconscious and silent way of telling themselves not to say too much. Even though Tiger Woods apologized for his cheating, his pursed lips indicated that there was a lot more he wasn't revealing; and indeed, more mistresses came forward following his speech.

Photo 8-20: Lance Armstrong pressing his lips together after being asked a question about his doping at a press conference. Photo credit: Jennifer Lorenzini/Splash News.

Lip biting

Sometimes people will bite their lips right before or as they tell a lie. When someone is telling you something and suddenly stops and bites her lower lip, chances are, she has just told you a lie or omitted pertinent information.

In this context, lip biting is a subconscious, self-protective signal to say no more. Right before Clinton apologized to the American people for lying about his affair with Monica Lewinksy, we could see him biting his lower lip as if to monitor what he was about to say. This facial language likely revealed that he didn't want to give away more information than he had to.

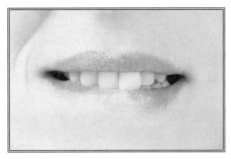

Photo 8-21: Lip biting is often a signal of deception.
Photo Credit: Marcell Mizik/ Shutterstock, Inc.

JAW MOVEMENT AND POSITIONING

The jutting jaw

Jaw movement and positioning are often telltale signals of deception. It can occur after the person has said something untrue. Oftentimes, after someone has lied, the jaw will jut forward as if in defiance. This can also happen when someone is angry about being questioned or doubted. We saw a clear example of this during O.J. Simpson's interview with Catherine Crier, when he was questioned about his wife Nicole's murder, on the 10-year anniversary of her death.

Photo 8-22: Note O.J. Simpson's jutting jaw as he is questioned about Nicole's death during an interview.
Photo credit: AdLIB Design/Splash News.

The dropped jaw

The jaw will often change position dramatically when someone has been caught in a lie. In those cases you can often see the jaw figuratively drop to the floor. The jaw drop can occur with the person's lips open or closed. The dropped jaw (with or without lips parted) is often an automatic reaction indicating surprise or shock. This isn't always from something negative, however (think of someone winning the lottery or seeing a long-lost relative after many years).

This jaw dropping was evident when *Today Show* reporter Meredith Viera bluntly asked "balloon dad" Richard Heene whether what had happened was a hoax. Richard was so taken off guard by her direct question that he literally dropped his jaw in surprise. When someone's lying is exposed, the jaw muscles may suddenly loosen and relax. The liar has literally lost control over his facial muscles as well as his lie. Lindsay Lohan exhibited a dropped jaw along with the wide eyes of surprise as she heard testimony in the Beverly Hills courthouse that may have exposed her lies to the judge.

Photo 8-23: Lindsay Lohan with mouth agape and the wide eyes of surprise after hearing something about herself in the courtroom that shocked her. Photo credit: Pool/London Entertainment/Splash News.

The jaw may also drop as the liar is lying. Here O.J. is speaking about what he would do if his teenage children ever asked him about Nicole's murder. What he said sounded so incredible and, frankly, unbelievable that it must have surprised even him.

Photo 8-24: O.J. Simpson with dropped jaw as he spins a story on Court TV on the 10-year anniversary of his wife Nicole's murder. Photo credit: AdLIB Design/Splash News.

Clenched jaw

You can often spot visible muscle tension in the jaw area when someone is being deceitful, or when he/she is angered or shocked by something. During the O.J. Simpson murder trial, we often saw O.J.'s lower jaw actually pulsate and his muscles tighten up when witness testimony hit too close to home. This tension comes from involuntarily biting down hard on the lower back teeth; the muscles tighten and often begin to pulsate or spasm. You will often see movement right under the cheekbone and about an inch away from the ear.

In this photo you can see Lance Armstrong's bulging facial muscles as he purses his lips and bites down on his back teeth. This indicates that he was feeling a great deal of tension and even anger—not surprising, really, considering that a reporter had just boldly questioned him about his doping. When their lies have been or are about to be exposed, many if not most liars will become angry. However, they need to mask those feelings in order to not give themselves away. Thus they may clench down on their back teeth in an attempt to control and mask their anger; ironically, however, this is exactly what reveals their anger and obvious deception. This facial language "tell" is often seen in the courtroom when a defendant lies or hears someone else accurately describing their misdeeds.

Photo 8-25: Lance Armstrong's clenched jaw and visible muscle tension indicating possible deception. Photo credit: Jennifer Lorenzini/Splash News.

RIGHTEOUS INDIGNATION

Whenever you see a flash of indignation that mocks and/or expresses anger, it is usually a clear signal of deception. Former Presidential candidate John Edwards made this expression when he discussed how he could not have possibly fathered a child by his mistress because of the timing. Likewise, when Richard Heene was asked if the whole story about his son being swept up in a hot air balloon was a hoax, his facial expression showed a flash of anger and indignation as he stated that he was getting "ticked off at these false accusations"—all of which later turned out to be true, of course.

O.J. Simpson also had this look of righteous indignation as he went on the offense during his Court TV interview. His indignant, almost mocking expression seems to scold the interviewer for even daring to question him about his wife's murder.

Photo 8-26: OJ Simpson showing facial "tell" of righteous indignation. Photo credit: AdLIB Design/Splash News.

Perhaps the most familiar example of righteous indignation can be seen in the historical photo of President Clinton with his pointed finger, narrowed eyes, and tight and angry jaw. His expression reflects that he feels offended that anyone could even think that he had sex with "that woman," Monica Lewinsky.

Photo 8-27: President Clinton's flash of icy righteous indignation. Photo credit: Joyce Naltchayan/DFP/Getty Images.

As always, when you scan someone's facial language for signs of deception, you must always keep in mind the context of what is being said (including the timing), as well as that person's baseline. "Tells" are essentially meaningless unless you have a good handle on all of these factors.

CHAPTER 9
THE VOICE OF A LIAR:
PITCH, VOLUME, TONE, AND PACING

I n this chapter you will discover how signals in the pitch, volume, tone (monotone or nasal), and pacing (slow and deliberate, or fast and "choppy") of someone's voice will tell you a tremendous amount about his or her personality and state of mind, and whether he/she is being truthful or not.

The voice is a barometer of how we feel about ourselves and the world around us. What we are thinking and feeling emerges through the tone of our voice, as well. You probably read peoples' voices all the time without even realizing it. When you answer the phone and someone close to you is on the other end, you can easily tell if that person is in a good mood or not. If it's your boss, you probably know right away if something is wrong at the office. In fact, we can pick up on most people's emotional states this way with a great deal of accuracy.

When we listen to someone speak and process what he has said and how he has said it (through our auditory cortex), the information is then passed to the limbic system, which controls and processes emotions. In turn we often mirror or react to the other person's emotion(s). The voice is an often subconscious conduit of our thoughts and feelings. For example, when you tell someone great news and hear a monotone voice replying, "That's nice; I'm happy for you," chances are, he's probably *not* all that happy for you.

PITCH

High pitch

An excessively high-pitched voice is often a sign of someone who is tentative, weak, and insecure. It can also be a signal of deception. This is especially true when a grown woman sounds like a 12-year-old girl, with a high-pitched, babyish voice. She may be purposefully misrepresenting herself in order to create an illusion of a sweet and innocent childlike person, when in reality this may not be the case.

A high-pitched voice can also indicate tension and even anger. Indeed, research shows that when we are angry, the pitch of our voice rises. Hence, it stands to reason that if someone constantly speaks in a high-pitched voice, she may be harboring a great deal of internal anger. She may even be angry at you for doubting what she has said or questioning whether she is being truthful. Therefore a rise in pitch can be a "tell" for deception and righteous indignation—anger over the perceived injustice of you not believing her. It is important to note that not all people with high-pitched voices are liars. Depending on the context and the person's baseline, however, it may be someone to be aware of.

Low pitch

While some people do have low voices based on the size and shape of their vocal anatomy, there are those people who will purposely make it a point to lower their voice for effect. Men who do this may want to be seen as sexier and more virile. They may also be (over-) compensating for some type of insecurity, especially if they don't always speak this way. The low-pitched voice may be a ploy, a way of misrepresenting themselves to appear more powerful or successful so that others will take them more seriously. But what they don't realize is that doing this often has the opposite effect, and only serves to make them look insecure, phony, or desperate/trying too hard.

If you're into Internet dating and you speak to a prospective date over the phone, and you hear either a very high or very low-pitched voice, know that the other person on the other end of the line may misrepresenting who they really are.

VOLUME

Speaking too softly

Those who speak too quietly, such that others constantly ask them to speak up, tend to have passive-aggressive personality traits and are often trying to manipulate others by forcing them to pay attention in a type of power play. By pretending they are gentle and delicate they are often able to gain control and manipulate you in a sneaky way. Those who speak so softly that you can barely hear them are usually carrying a big stick: they are usually full of hidden anger. A case in point was Ponzi schemer Bernard Madoff. While he was said to be an excellent listener, he was also said to be so soft-spoken that people were constantly asking him to speak up. No doubt he did this to gain control over others and, eventually, their money. He manipulated people by forcing them to ask him to speak up, as well as by letting them be the ones to ask, and in some cases beg him to be a part of his investment program.

These soft-spoken folks are liars because they are not who they appear to be. Their anger over whatever injustices they have experienced—being ignored, not feeling special or worthy in this world—is hidden in the soft tones they wield so that people will listen to them, so that they will finally feel a sense of importance. So if you find yourself constantly telling someone to speak up, you may want to leave him behind and associate only with those people whom you can hear. If not, you may eventually discover that this erstwhile timid, shy, demure, innocent-sounding, soft-spoken person is more than capable of being heard, particularly when he unexpectedly flies off the handle with a loud, booming voice and releases all of the pent-up anger that's been stored within him for so long.

Speaking too loudly

Like those who speak too softy, those who speak too loudly are also misrepresenting themselves. They crave attention, too, but they get it in a completely different way. They fairly force their presence upon you with their booming tones, whether you like it or not. These people tend to be arrogant, pompous, controlling, competitive, and bullying. Their anger surfaces regularly, in loud tones meant to manipulate and induce fear.

Oftentimes when people speak loudly they are compensating for something they know is not true. That is why people who lie often speak more loudly, as their subconscious aim is to convince others to believe them. If it's loud, it must be true! How many salespeople have you met who have tried to or have even succeeded in selling you a bill of goods by intimidating you? When you look back on these experiences, you will realize that it was not only their fast-talking, sweet-talking, bouncy tones that lured you in; it was their loud voice that made them seem larger than life. It's an attempt to manipulate and intimidate, in hopes that you will be more likely to part with your money. Unless someone has a hearing loss, if she's talking too loudly, it's likely she's trying to manipulate you with a raised voice. If she becomes louder and louder as she tries to convince you of something, there is a good chance she's being untruthful.

Before he was put in jail for what will likely be the rest of his life for armed robbery and kidnapping, O.J. Simpson's loud, lying voice could be heard periodically in the infamous 911 calls as well as in interviews as he discussed everything from his minor run-ins with the law to complaints about his then girlfriend, Christine Prody. O.J.'s craving for attention was not only reflected in his actions (not being able to stay out of trouble), but also in his loud, booming voice as he tried to convince anyone and everyone that nothing was his fault. The more he was questioned, it seemed, the louder he spoke.

Fading out

Fading or dying out at the ends of sentences is often a telltale sign of a liar. Remember that when we lie, our autonomic nervous system kicks in. Our body knows when we are lying, so it tries to shut down the lie on a physical level. The concurrent breathing changes make it difficult for us to get the words to flow out smoothly. As well, our throat muscles may tighten up when we speak, which results in a lack of sufficient air pressure. So if you are consistently unable to hear what someone says when they get to the ends of their sentences, know that his "swallowed" words may be an indicator that he is lying about something.

This phenomenon was evident when Bernard Madoff spoke to his clients. According to many who knew him, by the time this already soft-spoken, unassuming master manipulator got to the end of a sentence, one could barely hear him at all. On a conscious level, he knew all along that he was lying to investors, while subconsciously, his body (his vocal cord muscles) were trying to shut him down by closing off when he spoke. But people only became more intrigued by his soft-spoken manner.

TONE

A creaky or raspy tone

The same factors that cause the liar to die off at the ends of his sentences will often cause a creaky-sounding voice, as well. Whenever I watch deposition tapes as part of my consultations with attorneys and I hear someone with a creaky-sounding voice, it is often a red flag to me that they may not be telling the truth. The tense and tight muscles in the throat and voice box create a telltale raspy or creaky tone. This unappealing tone is the result of the body's way of "choking off" the lie. When Lance Armstrong went on *Oprah* and allegedly came clean, the audible vocal creakiness during specific parts of the interview may have indicated that he was being dishonest or at least withholding truthful information.

This creaky tone is also typically heard when someone has been caught in a lie. Before he was sentenced to death row, wife and unborn baby killer Scott Peterson was asked by a reporter what his girlfriend, Amber Frey, had said when he called her on the 24th. His voice creaked and rasped as he lied and denied ever calling her on the 24th. For her part, Amber claimed that he had in fact called her on the 24th and told her he was going to Belgium. In a creaky, barely audible voice, Scott then stated he was not going to waste any more precious time talking about it during the little time they had for the interview.

During his *Today Show* interview, ex-police officer Drew Peterson's voice changed dramatically when host Matt Lauer said:

> *People who have observed this case either from close in or outside say, "Drew, look—you have this devoted mom, you can't explain why she takes off, and you have the situation with your third wife, Kathleen Savio. Her body was exhumed. The death changed from an accidental death, following the autopsy, to homicide." And they look at you and say a year later, sitting on the couch here at the* Today Show, *[that] you've gotten away with at least one if not two murders. Do you understand why people feel that way?*

Drew Peterson was so stunned by the direct question that he could barely squeek out a reply. You could almost hear his vocal cords close off as looked away and creaked out, "I understand very well, as the media has done everything they can to keep me in a position looking guilty." Pause. "Appearing guilty." Similarly, when he was asked about the deceptive responses on his polygraph, his voice continued to crack as he said he didn't know why this had happened and had no knowledge of how a polygraph worked.

A shaky voice

When people are nervous, upset, angry, or unsure of something, it is not uncommon to hear a shakiness or a tremor in their voice when they speak. This occurs because the muscles in the throat systematically tighten up and relax, tighten up and relax, resulting in the tremulous, shaky tone. In contrast, with a creaky tone, the throat muscles don't relax at all.

This alternating tightening and relaxing of the vocal muscles can be an indication of deception. That is why so many people comment that they are bad liars; they give themselves away with their shaky voice. Of course, not all people who speak with a shaky voice are liars. They may have a neurological condition, or they may be taking medications that cause this as a side effect. Again, it's all about establishing a baseline—what's normal for that particular person—and then evaluating any deviations from that baseline with the greater context in mind.

Constant throat clearing

When someone constantly clears his throat, he either has chronic post-nasal drip or he's lying. As we already know, the liar's autonomic nervous system kicks into full gear, causing minute changes in blood flow and muscle tension. As his throat muscles tense up, it becomes more and more difficult for him to make sounds without it causing discomfort. The irritated feeling forces him to automatically clear his throat by bearing down on their throat muscles.

The more throat-clearing noises you hear, the more likely it is that someone is lying to you. When ex-police officer Drew Peterson went on his national television and radio tour claiming that he didn't know the whereabouts of his missing wife, Stacy, and that he didn't kill his third wife, Kathleen, he could be heard constantly clearing his voice. As it turned out, Drew was convicted of killing his third wife, and law enforcement is still looking into the possibility that he may have killed his fourth wife.

Attacking tones

People who "attack" their words with sudden bursts of volume are usually angry. They may be angry because they are feeling frustrated in their attempts to convince you of something, and are using attacking tones in an attempt to intimidate and control. Someone like this may also be feeling competitive with or jealous of you. The bottom line is that many of these vocal attackers, deep down, don't really like you; after all, it's hard to like someone when you are too busy feeling competitive or jealous of them.

Having a conversation with someone like this can be a jarring experience, peppered with little shocks of hostility, anger, and even hatred toward you. Even though this person may be saying nice words, the underlying hostile, attacking tone reveals how negatively he or she really feel toward you. Thus it is essential to not only pay close attention to what people say, but also the tone in which they say it; *this* is what will tell you how they really feel.

Hoaxer Richard Heene (a.k.a. balloon dad) was actually a very competitive person. He was constantly coming up with ideas to compete in the television market so that he and his family members could become celebrities. He also seemed to have anger issues, which was more than evident when he was on the television show *Wife Swap*; he actually became violent, throwing things at the "swapped" wives. All of this was reflected in and expressed in his typically harsh, attacking tone.

The nasal, whiny tone of the victim

When you hear a nasal, whiney tone that makes someone sound like a victim, know that you are likely being manipulated. Perpetual victims complain and whine in order to create drama and get attention. They will also often manipulate by being overly critical, in order to feel as though they have the upper hand and a sense of superiority over others.

There is often a defensive note in the tones of those who whine and constantly express their dissatisfaction. It is though they have a chip on their shoulder. They are critical of people and dislike them because, deep down, they really don't like themselves. They criticize and whine about others in order to elevate their low sense of self-worth. They are experts at blaming everyone but themselves and making themselves the victim in order to manipulate sympathy from others and to avoid being accountable for their own actions. Don't be naïve. Know that those who constantly criticize and whine about others will eventually turn around and do the same thing to you.

Although Lindsay Lohan often has a low, hoarse voice (perhaps due to smoking or abusing her voice), there is a victim-like, nasal, whiney quality to her voice as well. She seems to whine and complain about everything that goes wrong in her life without ever taking full accountability for her actions. Her parents assume the same nasal whine whenever they talk to the press and blame everyone else for their daughter's woes—except, of course, their toxic parenting or (perish the thought) their own daughter's actions. Know that whenever you hear this type of voice, you will rarely hear the truth.

A dull and lifeless monotone

A monotone can indicate an emotional state such as sadness or depression. If someone always sounds like this, he or she may be chronically depressed. People who "put on" a monotone, on the other hand, are usually trying to keep their emotional distance from others. However, they'll turn on the charm and pull you in when they want something. These vocally ungenerous people never want others to know their true feelings; they fear being found out, so they use a noncommittal tone to keep others at bay and in the dark. Speaking with these people can be very frustrating and exhausting because they don't give you any feedback. You have no access to their true and honest thoughts and feelings, which would allow for a genuine conversation. Conversations with such people are rarely reciprocal, as they tend not to reveal personal information or anything of an emotional nature. Being on the receiving end of this lack of reciprocity can feel a bit sneaky. You may find it very difficult to trust someone like this, and for the most part, you'd be right.

When Tiger Woods apologized to his fans and to his family for his cheating, his emotionless monotone made many doubt the sincerity of his feelings. Many felt was just going through the motions because he did not want to lose any more commercial endorsements. His robotic and mechanical body movements actually matched his stiff and insincere speech patterns.

Many psychopaths/sociopaths speak in this kind of dull tone. Of course, not all people who sound like this are sociopaths, but at the very least, know that their superficial communication style is making it impossible for you to communicate your deepest thoughts and feelings. As a result, there tends to be more miscommunication, misunderstanding, and mistrust with and among these people, as you are never have access to their emotions and thus can never be sure what their intentions are.

A sugary-sweet tone

No one is nice and happy and cheery *all* the time, so if you come across someone who is—run. Run as fast as you can and as far away as possible.

Most often these people are highly passive aggressive and harbor a lot of anger. Their chronic sugary sweetness is usually a mask for how they really feel, deep inside. They are often sneaky and use their sweet tones to gather information from others and turn it against them, or use that information for their own benefit. In this sense they are the most manipulative of all liars.

People with this kind of voice can turn on you in a moment's notice, so pay close attention to any double messages, inconsistencies, and incongruent behaviors. When they do finally let out their anger, their unctuous tones will turn bitter in the blink of an eye, and the barrage of vitriol can be head-spinning. So beware. This was certainly the case with boyfriend killer Jodi Arias. Most people who thought they knew her described her as "sweet" and kind. In fact, upon first meeting her, many of her now deceased boyfriend's friends, family members, and associates asked him if Jodi was always that sweet. What they didn't know was that behind that sweetness hid a woman who was full of pent-up rage and capable of murdering someone she claimed to love.

PACING AND CADENCE

Fast, frenetic speech

When someone sounds like a cheerleader all the time, overly upbeat and chipper, oftentimes this can be a manipulative ploy. It probably seems as though everything she says and does has a sense of urgency to it: it has to be done *now*. She probably tends to enroll you in her projects and schemes, when you really have no intention of participating. Her excited, upbeat tone (which often also carries with it a sense of alarm) is meant to make you hop to it. If she is always excited and enthusiastic, it can be contagious.

The good news is that these upbeat, enthusiastic, fast-talking people can be great motivators—as they cheer you on in your diet or exercise regime, for example. But they can also be incredibly manipulative and controlling when they rope you into doing something that is only for their benefit. Usually their lives are filled with crisis after crisis, and they need *your* help in solving their problems. Because they sound so cheery and convincing, it is all too easy to fall for their lies; after all, you want to help.

The bottom line is that these people can be lethal if you allow them to control and manipulate you into becoming their puppet. Never agree to do what they want, when they want it done. Take your time to process everything, and certainly, don't allow them to convince you to do something you don't want to do. Don't let them manipulate you, and refuse to get involved in any of their schemes, any of which will likely cost you time or money or both.

Know that most people who sound like this tend to be not only highly manipulative but selfish, as well. They also have few or no boundaries, as they have to be the center of attention and in control of everything and everyone. Think of yourself first, because they certainly won't. Constantly set boundaries so you will not fall prey to their lies and manipulations. They cannot be compassionate or sensitive to your needs, since it is all about them. Above all, don't let their sense of urgency tyrannize you. Take your time to process everything they say so that you won't feel used or manipulated.

"Balloon dad" Richard Heene also had this hyper-frenetic way of talking as he tried to convince everyone to buy his lame-brained schemes, everything from taking his kids into storm-chasing areas to convincing the world his son was floating away in a hot air balloon. Even as he admitted to the world that it had been a hoax, he still continued to make excuses and deceive in that same frenetic tone, even after he was released from jail.

Staccato, choppy cadence

Those who over-articulate or speak in a choppy, deliberate manner usually tend to be rigid, self-righteous, and inflexible. Because it is difficult for them to bend and compromise, they usually can't just go with the flow. They resemble admonishing grade-school teachers who speak to children in short, simple sentences with exaggerated enunciation. They tend to use this staccato, self-righteous tone to intimidate others and make themselves right.

Someone who suddenly speaks in this choppy, hyper-articulated cadence may be lying. Oftentimes a key to recognizing deception is when someone suddenly stops speaking with a flowing cadence or stops using contractions, such as "didn't" or "isn't." A person who is lying will most likely say "No, I did not do that" instead of "No, I didn't do it." This type of communication is a very common "tell" when analyzing statements of those involved in criminal acts. As I listened to Bernard Madoff's voice as he issued his apology to the court, I was struck by the hyper articulation, the overemphasis of words, and the overall choppiness of his delivery. It sounded as though he were mocking and taunting his victims through these very deliberately pronounced words and sounds. Similarly, when he lied to the public, President Clinton didn't say "I didn't have sex with that woman"; instead, he said "I did not have sex with that woman." Thus, when someone suddenly becomes formal and doesn't use contractions, it is often a signal that they are not telling the truth.

Stuttering and stammering

Not everyone who has a stammer or stutter is a liar, of course. It could be a simple matter of having a speech impediment. But when someone who usually doesn't stutter, suddenly begins to stumble over his or her words, it is a huge "tell" for deception, particularly if he/she is stumbling over crucial or significant information.

Slow, deliberate speech

Like those who speak too quickly, those who speak too slowly are often self- absorbed, uncaring, and/or unaware others' reactions to their delivery style. Oftentimes this is because they either don't pay attention to or care about the feelings of others. I am not talking about Southerners who draw out their words or phrases, or those who have a legitimate physiological condition that causes slow and labored speech. Nor am I talking about those who speak slowly because they are on a certain a medication or medications. Instead I am referring to a way of speaking that is purposely used to manipulate and control. People who speak this way on purpose do so to make sure you are paying attention and that you are listening to every. Single. Syllable. If you try to interrupt them or hurry them along, they will often ignore you and continue to speak over you, ignoring your wishes and instead insisting on finishing their message, whatever it was.

Bernard Madoff spoke in this slow, labored manner when he gave his "apology" statement to the court before he was hauled off to prison for life. He not only over-articulated every word, as we learned earlier in this chapter, but he spoke slowly and deliberately in his attempt to have one last opportunity to exert even a modicum of control over others. It was likely the last he would ever taste of this, since he was going to spend the rest of his life in prison.

Nervous laughter

If you hear someone telling a story and consistently hear them laugh at times when it is not appropriate to laugh they may be displaying anxiety or nervousness. Their anxiety and nervousness could also be due to the fact that they are telling a lie. Oftentimes their sudden bursts of inappropriate laughter is an uncontrollable reaction designed to mask their lie. The limbic system, located deep in the brain controls emotion, including happiness and joy which manifests through laughter. But when a person lies, their true emotion which may be anxiety, nervousness, and in some cases fear surfaces. In an attempt to quickly mask those genuine emotions, the person will force a laugh.

One of the ways you can tell a phony and nervous laugh is that it doesn't last long, occurs with frequency, and the transition to a serious facial expression is quick. When a person genuinely laughs, when they recover from their laugh you will usually see a smile on their face before they transition into a serious expression. With the lying nervous laugh you won't see that smile. Instead they will go from the laugh straight to a serious facial expression.

CHAPTER 10

SPEECH CONTENT: IT'S NOT JUST WORDS

W e've already seen *how* people say things—their body language—is crucial in determining whether they are telling the truth. Now we will discuss *what* liars say, the specific verbal cues that can let you know if you are in the presence of a liar. Just as someone's true emotions and intentions can leak out through their body language, facial language, and vocal patterns, they can also leak out through what they actually say. Following are some major communication "tells" to look for that can help you assess whether someone is being truthful with you or not.

TOO MUCH INFORMATION, TALKING TOO MUCH, AND GOING OFF ON TANGENTS

When someone goes on and on and gives you way too much information— information that is not requested and especially an excess of details—there is a very high probability that he or she is not telling you the truth. Liars often talk a lot because they are hoping that, with all their talking and seeming openness, others will believe them. Former Court TV host Catherine Crier said this after she interviewed O.J. Simpson on the 10th anniversary of his wife, Nicole's murder. After the very lengthy interview with him, Catherine stated that said it was her opinion that O.J. talks a lot because he feels that people will believe him.

Catherine is absolutely correct, as most people who lie tend toward excess verbosity in order to try to sound more convincing. However, in talking a lot, they often inadvertently give away some pretty significant information—sometimes even the truth. O.J. Simpson continued his pattern of talking a lot when he spoke to the Las Vegas court before his sentencing in 2008. Here is a part of the actual transcript, with my interpolations in brackets:

> *I don't want to hurt Bruce. And I didn't want to hurt any of these guys. I know these guys. These guys have eaten in my home [tangent]. I've done book reports with their kids [tangent]. I sung [sic] to their mothers when they've been sick [tangent]. You know I wasn't there to hurt anybody. I wanted my personal things and I realize now that was stupid of me. I'm sorry I didn't mean to steal anything from anybody and I didn't know I was doing anything illegal, I was confronting friends.*

Clearly, Judge Jackie Glass didn't think confronting friends with a gun was all that friendly and sentenced him to prison for armed robbery.

Former President George W. Bush provided a bit too much tangential information as he told an audience about his experiences during 9/11. Virtually the entire world saw the President sitting in a children's classroom as he was told the news of the attack. As an aide whispered in his ear, he bit his lip, indicating that he didn't want to say anything in front of the children. In a speech three months after the attack, however, he described the scene as follows: "I was sitting outside the classroom waiting to go in and I saw an airplane hit the tower, uh, of a TV, uh—the TV was obviously on." (We all saw that there was no TV on anywhere when he was told about the attack.)

The two main signals of deception were these: he volunteered too much extraneous information (about the television being on); and he used the word *obviously* when he said "the TV was obviously on." If someone had actually been watching TV that day and were in genuine shock over the tower being hit, he or she would not have used the word *obviously* or even mentioned a TV being on. These needless, tangential details were indicative of someone who was not being completely truthful.

The President then went off on a tangent and said, " I used to fly myself, and I said, *Now, there's one terrible pilot*. And, uh, then I said it must have been a horrible accident, but I was whisked off...and didn't have much time to think about it." We all saw that the President had not been "whisked off"; in fact, he remained seated in the classroom for a few moments, which gave him at least some time to think about what had happened. In my opinion, what Bush said during this part of his speech was less than truthful.

Sometimes a liar will bring up the truth all on his own. For example, when Jennifer asked Ken where he was last night, instead of saying he was with friends or at the movies and leaving it at that, he said he was at the movies and *would never cheat on her*. Jennifer wasn't even thinking about him cheating on her—until he brought it up. Later she came to find out that he had indeed cheated on her that evening, when he said he had been at the movies not cheating on her.

DEFLECTING AND BLAMESHIFTING

When you hear someone constantly blame others, it can be a huge red flag that he or she is lying. Instead of coming clean about what really happened, people like this try to deflect the truth. A clear example of this was Lance Armstrong's interview with Oprah. He refused to accept the fact that what he had done was wrong, and in fact he harbored no guilt about it. He seemed to blame everyone for his misdeeds but himself. He first blamed the culture, his fans, and even his story, the story of a cyclist who had beaten cancer and won the competition. He blamed his cancer for having made him so driven. He blamed his mother for being a fighter and for making him into a fighter. He even blamed fellow cyclist Floyd Landis for uncovering the whole scandal; in Armstrong's opinion, Landis had done this as a way to get back at him after having been banned from the cycling team.

Liars who blameshift like this believe that nothing is their fault. Even hours before she was to be executed for multiple counts of murder, serial killer Aileen Wuornos continued to lie about her role in the murders and even justify what she had done. She insisted that everything was the police's fault, society's fault, and the court's fault. Likewise, when President Clinton first denied his affair with Monica Lewinsky, he and his aides blamed the press for making up and perpetuating the story. Perhaps the biggest blamershifters we see in the media are the parents of troubled famous children. Lindsay Lohan's parents seem to blame everyone but Lindsay for her bad behavior.

FILLER WORDS: "UHS," "LIKES," "UMS," AND "YOU KNOWS"

If you hear someone use a lot of these kinds of useless filler words, chances are he or she is lying. Richard Heene did this when he claimed that his son had been carried away in a balloon but had been found safe, hiding in an attic. On camera, CNN interviewer Wolf Blitzer assured Heene that he was just trying to clarify what Heene's son Falcon had meant by his comment that "we [the Heene family] did this for the show." Richard Heen's response was as follows:

> *Well, you know, we were on* Wife Swap *a couple of times, so the camera crews out there...I would imagine that they'd ask him a couple of questions in reference to this and, uh, I believe you know he meant, uh, something to do with that.*

In this case, the awkward, repetitive use of these filler words reflected Richard Heene's deception.

WORDS THAT DEMAND REASSURANCE AND REFERENCE HONESTY

"Do you know what I mean?" "Are you with me?" "Do you hear me?" "Are you following what I am saying?" These are the phrases liars will often use to check in with you, to get reassurance that you are still listening and on board. These liars are essentially fishing for words of reassurance so that they know it's safe to continue with their lie. This reassurance and confirmation gives them confidence and emboldens them further.

If they don't get this reassurance right away, they will continue to badger you until they do. If you remain silent or question them, they will often become confrontational and defensive. When hoaxer Richard Heene began rattling off his explanation on CNN as to why his young son would say that they "did it [the balloon scare] for show," he opened by saying, "Well, you know...." Typically when people use this phrase before they answer a question, chances are, they are lying. Likewise, when people are honest, they don't have to tell you they are honest. So when someone uses words and phrases such as, "Honestly," "I have to be honest with you," "To tell you the truth," "Truthfully," "I swear," or "You know I am being perfectly honest," understand that he or she is attempting to convince you of his or her honesty. Know, too, that there's a high probability that he/she is hiding something.

FLATTERY, COMPLIMENTS, AND OBSEQUIOUSNESS

While everyone likes compliments and hearing nice things about themselves, when someone gives you too many compliments or makes too many ingratiating or obsequious comments, he usually wants something from you. In Bernard Madoff's case, it was other peoples' money, but only if you had a lot of it. Other swindlers don't care how much money you have. They want every last cent of whatever is yours. They even want the money that isn't yours. They will cajole, flatter, and make you feel like a million bucks just so they can tap into your finances. Have you ever received one of those bogus emails from Nigeria claiming that someone left you a fortune and all he needs you to do is release the money from your bank account? Those sorts of phishing scams are usually filled with flattering comments.

Those who knew Bernard Madoff remarked that he was very complimentary of others and made people feel good about themselves—something he understood very well. He could make the other person feel as though he or she were the most interesting, intelligent, successful, attractive person in the world. Since many of his clients were high-powered businesspeople and professionals who had healthy egos to begin with, he only had to play into that. He played verbal music to their ears, and they loved it. In fact, one reporter who visited him in prison commented afterward that he made her feel like the most accomplished reporter in the world. So if you are hearing a lot of kind and flattering words—some of which may ring true and some which may not—know that this is often a huge red flag that you're dealing with a con artist or a liar.

AVOIDING CONTRACTIONS

Most people feely use contractions in order to make their speech "flow" better and sound less stilted. Liars, on the other hand, avoid using contractions, instead saying each word separately to stress that they. Are. Not. Lying. Note that President Clinton didn't say "I didn't have sex with that woman"; instead, he said, "I did not have sex with that woman." Likewise, when a reporter confronted Scott Peterson about calling his girlfriend, Amber Frey, he replied, "No, I did not." When someone suddenly stops using contractions as he denies something, know that he is probably lying.

INCORRECT VERB TENSES

Liars will often confuse their tenses. For example, they will refer to something in the past as though it were happening in the present. O.J. Simpson did this when he was speaking with journalist Catherine Crier. He used the present tense when he discussed an event that had already occurred. Psychopaths/sociopaths often confuse their tenses, as well. Research has indicated that this may be a result of their neurological functioning and cognitive processes.

REPEATING THE QUESTION AND GIVING EVASIVE ANSWERS

When reporter Bob Costas interviewed Jerry Sandusky, he asked him point blank, "Are you a sexually attracted to young boys?" In a very slow, drawling speech, drawing out all of his syllables, Sandusky answered by repeating the question: "Am I sexually attracted to young boys?" His answer spoke for itself. He essentially admitted that he was indeed a child molester. Sandusky further implicated himself by repeating, "Sexually attracted? No, no. I enjoy young people. I love to be around them, um, I, uh, not, I'm not [pause] sexually attracted to young boys..." as his voice trailed off.

When you ask a liar a direct question, it is not uncommon to hear him repeat the question before answering. For example: "Where was I last night? I was at Pete's house helping him...." Then, he may follow that with an evasive answer, such as, "Well, I was anywhere and everywhere last night." This guy is lying. Repeating the question is a way of buying time so that the liar can think up an answer that will pass muster.

INCONSISTENCIES

People who tell the truth are consistent. The beginning, middle, and end of the story is always the same, no matter how many times they tell it, to whom they tell it, or when they tell it. Liars, on the other hand, often have a hard time with this. They will change their stories, embellish them, or omit significant details. This is one of the biggest and most obvious signs that someone is not telling the truth.

DEFENSIVENESS AND CONTENTIOUSNESS

A therapist received a phone call from a man claiming to be the union boss from the Screen Actors Guild. He wanted to send her Screen Actors Guild clients something, but then, on almost the next breath, he said he wanted some information from her. She politely told him that she wasn't interested and hung up the phone. The man called back moments later and started putting her down, asking her what was wrong with her and telling her that he was trying to do her a favor. After admonishing her for hanging up on him he gave her an 800 number to call. She said she would have to think about it. After hanging up and giving it some thought, she realized that he had called from a number with a 702 area code. She typed the number on her caller ID into her computer and found that it was from a call center in Las Vegas that was trying to scam business professionals.

When someone is cheating on his mate, it is not uncommon for him to turn the tables and accuse his spouse of being the one who is cheating. If some becomes hostile and defensive upon being asked a question, saying, "Why are you asking me that?" and accuses *you* of wrongdoing, he is usually lying.

We clearly saw this defensive table-turning on CNN when anchor Wolf Blitzer asked Richard Heene about his son's statement:

> *Earlier in the show I asked you to relay the question to Falcon that he was hiding in the garage for about four hours, and I asked you to ask him why he didn't come out after he heard you and his mom and everyone else screaming for [him], and you said to him, "Falcon why didn't you come out?" And Falcon said, "Um, you guys said that, um, we did this for the show." And you said, "Um." What did he mean, "we did this for the show"?*

> *Richard reluctantly turned to Falcon and there was a long, awkward pause. He then said, "They want to know why you were in the attic and why you waited so long to, uh...." Then Richard paused and said to Blitzer, "Uh, say, say it again," at which point Blitzer repeated the question. Richard then paused and said,*

> *Uh, [let me] interrupt this real quick because I can see the direction you guys are hedging [sic] on this because earlier you had asked the police officers a question, uh, the media out front, we weren't even gonna do this interview, um, and I'm kind of appalled after all the feelings [bites his lower lip] that I went through up and down that you guys are trying to suggest something else. Okay, I'm really appalled because they said out in front that this would be the end and I wouldn't have to be bothered with any other, so, uh, or anything. So we said okay, fine, we'll do this, so I'm kind of appalled that you guys would say something like that.*

Notice how Richard uses the word *appalled* three times during his statement, a display of righteous indignation.

RIGHTEOUS INDIGNATION

We can never forget the look on former President Clinton's face as he looked directly into the camera with narrowed eyes and tight jaw, or his body language as he pointed his finger at us. What was equally unforgettable was his admonishing preamble, "I am gonna say this again." When people say "You better listen to me" or "I don't care if you don't believe me" or "This is the honest truth," they are usually *not* telling the truth. It is all part and parcel of that righteous indignation that is common to almost all liars. They are angry and indignant that you would dare accuse them of lying, so they express it to you nonverbally as well as verbally. In Shakespeare's words, it is a case of "the lady doth protest too much," insisting assiduously and passionately that something is not true, to the extent that it must be true.

INCONGRUENT FACIAL EXPRESSION

When someone's words don't match his facial expression, and vice versa, you can be almost certain he is lying. This is where the integrity of someone's communication is crucial: you not only need to look at the person's body language, but match it up with his facial expression, his tone of voice, and what is actually being said. If things don't match up, rest assured that the person is lying.

Bernard Madoff stood up in court and said, "I apologize to my victims. I will turn and face you." He twisted his body to face his victims for one second and then, sounding as though he were reading from a stage script, said in a monotone, "I'm sorry. I know that doesn't help you," and immediately sat down. He was right. His "apology" didn't help anyone and in fact angered almost everyone who heard it. While the words were marginally comforting, the fact that they were spoken in an emotionless monotone negated everything he said. His victims felt he was being insincere and that his apology was a lie in that he demonstrated no remorse for what he had done.

Nodding when saying yes and vice versa

When you say yes or agree to something, your head will usually nod up and down in agreement. So, when O.J. Simpson shook his head back and forth as she said that he didn't know he was doing anything illegal when he took it upon himself to take his own property from memorabilia brokers, it was one of the few times that he was telling the truth that this was his actual thought at the time. But when Lance Armstrong said to Oprah, "I am flawed, deeply flawed," he shook his head, indicating that deep down he really didn't feel deeply flawed at all. In fact, at the beginning of the interview, when Oprah asked him if he thought what he did was wrong, he showed no signs of deception when he said no. When he told Oprah that what he had done was "inexcusable," he once again shook his head when he should have been nodding it in agreement, reflecting that the only thing that was inexcusable to him was the fact that had been caught.

STATEMENTS THAT SOUND LIKE QUESTIONS

When someone sounds as though she is asking a question when she is actually making statement, it is a good indication that she is lying. I am not referring to "uptalk" or Valley Girl speak or anything young people say to sound cool; they tend to consistently speak like this throughout their conversation. Instead, I am talking about a situation in which you suddenly hear this upward inflection in the middle of a conversation. In his interview on *Oprah*, for example, Lance Armstrong discussed Emma O'Reilly, a woman who had rightly accused him of taking cortisone and whom he sued. About her, he said, "She's one of these people I have to apologize to...?" with an upward inflection at the end. This meant that he likely didn't want to apologize to Emma.

TAKING TOO LONG TO ANSWER/OVERLY LONG PAUSES

If someone takes an inordinately long time to think of an answer, or pauses too long between words, chances are he or she is lying. This person is likely buying time as he/she is trying to think up a good answer. What was striking about Bob Costas's interview with Jerry Sandusky was how long it took Jerry to answer the questions that were posed to him. He should have been able to rattle off his answers immediately, not wait in awkward silence for several seconds before he answered. Unsurprisingly, it's since been confirmed that he was lying.

"I WAS ONLY KIDDING"

Many times people will inadvertently spill the truth (especially if it's something insulting about you) and then immediately try to negate or cancel it by adding, "I was only kidding." Know that in almost all cases, when someone says this, he or she is not kidding. The rude or sarcastic statement is exactly how they feel about you. They have just told you the truth, so believe them!

"I DON'T KNOW" AND "I DON'T RECALL"

If someone is constantly peppering their speech with "I don't know" or "I don't recall," chances are they actually *do* know. People who constantly use this phrase are usually nonconfrontational; they don't want to make waves or tell you what they are really thinking. So they play it safe by vacillating and constantly saying that they don't know. Oftentimes if you ask for their true opinion about something, they will use this response, even when they most definitely have an opinion. You hear this most often during election times when people don't want to tell you their real political views. So they will often lie by omission and say they don't know or haven't decided, when they really do know and have decided.

When Oprah asked Lance why he was coming forward now, when for 13 years he brazenly and defiantly denied everything he had just admitted on her show, he looked down and replied, "I don't know that I have a great answer." But in actuality, Lance knew why he chose to come clean and admit to doping: he still wanted to have the opportunity to compete in cycling races in the future.

MINIMIZING AND MAKING EXCUSES

When people are caught in a lie, they may continue to lie as they justify their behavior by minimizing their actions. Take Lance Armstrong's response to Oprah as he answered her question about his drug use:

My, uh, cocktails so to speak was, was, only, uh, E. P. O. [not a lot]—transfusions, then testosterone, which in a weird way I almost justified because of my history, obviously, because I have testicular cancer and losing...surely I'm running low.

Here we see how Lance justified his actions by telling us that he only took a little of one drug, and how he only took the other drug because of his testicular cancer. His minimizing statements and self-justification supported and continued the lie, even after he admitted to doping. Indeed, he admitted later in the interview that it was true what Emma O'Reilly had said about his taking yet another drug—cortisone.

DETACHING, REFERRING TO OTHERS AND SELF IN SECOND OR THIRD PERSON

When Lance Armstrong discussed how he had sued the people who exposed his doping, he said, "It's a flaw." Note that he didn't say, "I have a flaw." By referring to himself in the third person as "it," he was essentially detaching himself from his crime and putting distance between himself and what he had done. Tellingly, he went on to say "*It's a guy* who expected to get whatever he wanted and to control every outcome [italics mine]."

Another example of how someone detached during a lie could be seen in O.J. Simpson's Court TV interview with Catherine Crier. She and everyone else watching found it impossible to believe that in the 10 years since Nicole's death, O.J.'s teenaged children had never asked him about their mother's death, despite the fact that they had been in therapy. What gave him away was the fact that he detached and referred to himself as "you" when he described what he would say if they ever asked him about their mother. While pointing his index finger, he said, "The day they ask, no matter what you are doing, don't say *Wait 'til we get home.* Uh, no matter what you are doing, drop it, take them somewhere, and talk to them about it." When Catherine pressed the point and asked him what, specifically, he would say, since he had had 10 years to think about it, he responded by saying that "you couldn't tell them anything as fact, just how you felt." If he had been telling the truth, he would not have referred to himself in the second person.

FREUDIAN SLIPS

Liars will often tell the truth through a slip of the tongue, or Freudian slip. As I mentioned previously, the brain doesn't "want" to lie. Lies take a lot of effort. You have to think up a story and make it sound believable. Then, you have to remember the story and not contradict yourself. The brain and the body want to do what comes naturally and what is easy—namely, telling the truth. So it is not uncommon for the truth to leak out in one of these slips. That is why you have to listen carefully to what people say. If you ask your single, never-married boyfriend to follow you in your car and he says, "I'm a good father," when he meant to say, "I'm a good follower," you might want to look a little more deeply into his past.

Oftentimes after someone has betrayed himself in this manner, he will show signs of embarrassment as he rushes to correct his "error" and make all kinds of excuses for what he just said. That is yet another sign that he lied or has something to hide. So listen for slips of the tongue and unexpected kernels of truth that leak out of the mouth of the liar.

NONSENSICAL SPEECH

When people are caught in a lie, it is not uncommon to hear them speak in sentence fragments that don't seem to make any sense. They will ramble on or use inappropriate words. When Richard Heene was essentially busted by Wolf Blitzer, his response was, "I see where this is hedging," instead of "I see where this is heading." The reason liars mix up words or even make new ones up is because their brains have to work extra fast to do damage control. So their thoughts come out more quickly and, often, unintelligibly.

CHAPTER 11
YOUR LYING EYES:
LOVERS WHO CHEAT AND DECEIVE

You and your spouse were beside yourselves when you learned from a mutual friend that Jenny and Andy, the couple with whom you went out to dinner a week earlier, were getting a divorce. You have known the now-divorcing couple for years. You always thought they were so happy together, with a solid relationship. Certainly all seemed fine between them at dinner. You didn't notice any problems. Your spouse wants to know what happened but doesn't want to impose on them by asking. He figures they will call and tell you when they feel comfortable. On the other hand, you want to know *now*, so you pick up the phone and call Jenny's cell. Jenny breaks down and confesses to you how she finally got sick of Andy's controlling ways and how he puts her down all the time.

Now that she mentions it, you recall that he did belittle her and make her the brunt of his jokes. But you thought he was kidding, because that's what he always said: "Relax, I'm only kidding." But now that you replay some of the things he said to her that night at dinner, in retrospect, they did sound a bit mean-spirited. Then you thought about how he ordered for her and lightly slapped her wrist, telling her she couldn't have any more bread. Once again, you thought he was just kidding around. But as you think more deeply about the evening, you recall how they sat facing away from one another. They barely looked at one another. When she wanted desert, he told her to stop it. She shook her head and frowned. Again, you thought he was just being funny. After getting an earful from Jenny, however, you realize that there is nothing funny about their relationship. Apparently, she was living a nighmare.

Almost every day, it seems, I am called upon by some media outlet to determine whether certain newsmaker couples are genuinely happy or in trouble and on the path to breaking up. No matter how much spin their public relations team or their handlers put on it, if you know what signs to look for, you will never be fooled or surprised that someone's relationship is on the rocks. Sometimes people are even in denial regarding their *own* relationships and fail to see the signs until it is too late. You don't have to be one of those people.

Following are some of the body language "tells" that may indicate that a relationship is headed for disaster. Many of the celebrity couples you see in these photos were in troubled relationships that eventually ended. Even though they lied by insisting in the press that all was well between them, their body language told the truth, as you will discover. Even though I am showing you photos of celebrity couples, you will see many of these same "tells" in couples you know personally. You may even see them in your own relationship.

WALKING IN FRONT OF YOUR MATE

Unless you come from a culture or believe in a religion that says it's acceptable for a woman to walk many steps behind a man, this behavior can be a huge red flag that a relationship is in trouble. For years, actor Ashton Kutcher was always photographed in loving poses beside his wife, Demi, so it came as a huge surprise when photographs turned up showing him walking two to three steps ahead of her. In these photos he wasn't even acknowledging her presence. So it came as no surprise to me when their relationship finally ended a year after this particular photo was taken.

Photo 11-1: Ashton Kutcher walks two steps ahead of wife, Demi Moore, seemingly without acknowledging her presence. Photo credit: Ron Asadorian/Splash News.

When someone walks in front of you without grabbing your hand, it often means that he has lost interest in or respect for you, or just doesn't like you. His walking ahead of you literally means that he wants to get away from you.

LOOKING IN DIFFERENT DIRECTIONS

When couples are consistently looking in different directions it means that these two independent people are not like-minded and have their own agendas. Because these people are not in synch, it makes for a very difficult relationship in the long run. If this happens often, it can mean that the couple is simply mismatched.

Perhaps the most mismatched couple of all time was journalist and Kennedy family member Maria Shriver and Austrian body builder Arnold Schwarzenegger. They were culturally, politically, religiously, and, as it turned out, morally different. Maria finally filed for divorce after it was revealed to the world that Arnold not only cheated on her with their housekeeper, but had also had an illegitimate son with her. Although Arnold ended up acknowledging the boy and supported him financially, the incident only served to magnify their differences.

Since the beginning of their relationship, these two were rarely photographed looking in the same direction, This means they were not like-minded. From their dating years, their wedding photos, and their attending numerous public events, to the time Arnold was governor of California and Maria was the first lady, they rarely looked in the same direction in photos. To me this signified that the couple literally looked at life differently, and it was no surprise that they eventually ended up going in different directions.

Photo 11-2: Arnold Schwarzenegger and Maria Shriver looking in different directions. Photo credit: Mario Anzuoni/Splash News.

TOO MUCH SPACE, TOO LITTLE CONTACT

When a couple is first dating, engaged to be married, or recently married, you should be seeing a lot of physical displays of affection between them; if not, the couple is headed for trouble. After looking at countless photographs and videos of Kim Kardashian and Kris Humphries, I could see a marked lack of love and affection. I noticed this even before they tied the knot in their lavish television ceremony for what I considered a loveless wedding, one that lasted only 72 days. There is a great deal of physical distance between them in almost all of their many photos together. They rarely touched, and any attempts at touching one another appeared awkward and uncomfortable. This was likely the result of a lack of physical chemistry.

Photo 11-3: Note the physical distance and obvious lack of affection between Kim Kardashian and Kris Humphries. Photo credit: VLUV/Splash News.

After their over-the-top televised wedding ceremony, I was interviewed by the press about their body language, and I was the first to predict the demise of their relationship. They appeared awkward and unaffectionate, certainly nothing like a couple in love who couldn't keep their hands off of one another. The dynamic between them on their reality show was even more distant. On the show I saw signs that the relationship would not last; from the way they spoke to one another to the way they looked at one another and even stood and sat near one another, it was no surprise to me and many others that they finally parted ways. I am guessing it was probably a relief to them, as well.

Here is a photo of Tiger Woods and Elin Nordegren shortly after the scandal of his infidelity broke, and when they were attempting to reconcile their marriage. Note the extreme physical distance between them. The fact that she is looking down and not at Tiger was another bad sign for the marriage. Indeed, they were unable to fully reconcile and ultimately divorced.

Photo 11-4: Note the physical distance between Tiger Woods and Elin Nordegren. This photo was taken during the time they were trying to save their marriage, which subsequently ended in divorce. Photo: Splash News.

FEET POINTING IN THE WRONG DIRECTION

There were countless signs of distress in Katie Holmes and Tom Cruise's relationship throughout the years—if you knew what to look for. Whenever I told the press what I observed in their body language, Tom's fans were not too happy about it. In their emails they would insist that Tom and Katie's relationship was ideal. But nothing could convince *my* eyes.

I clearly saw the demise of their relationship well ahead of time. In fact, I saw serious signs of unhappiness in Katie's body language six months before she finally had the nerve to secretly gather her belongings and move out their home to begin a new life on the east coast, along with their school-aged daughter, Suri.

Photo 11-5: "Feet giveaways" in Katie Holmes and Tom Cruise's body language at the premiere of *Mission Impossible: Ghost Protocol*. Photo credit: Lakota/Splash News.

As you can see in this photo, in addition to her tense facial expression and the fact that she's looking in the opposite direction and literally pulling her body away from him, there is a lot of information about Katie's disdain for Tom in the position of her feet. Her toes are pointed inward, giving them a pigeon-toed appearance. While Katie's body language reveals that she doesn't care for Tom, Tom's body language says the opposite, that he really likes/loves her. In contrast, his toes are pointed in her direction and he leans his body into her, all the while maintaining an open body position. He also has a calm and pleasant look on his face, with a relaxed jaw. On the other hand, Katie's lower jaw and facial muscles appear very tense.

After looking at this photo and several similar photos of the two of them together, it is easy to understand how Tom must have been shocked when he finally learned how miserable Katie was in their relationship and that she was desperate to leave him. Based on his positive feelings toward Katie as reflected in his body language, Tom obviously had no clue that something was wrong. But had he really examined the photos of the two of them together throughout the years and analyzed how Katie's body language appeared when she was around him, he may have been able to spot trouble on the horizon.

COMPETITION: HOGGING THE LIMELIGHT

When couples are in a competitive relationship for whatever reason, it often shows up in their body language when they are together. One will try to outdo the other, which ultimately ends up destroying the love between them. When two people have formidable careers and they aren't supportive of one another, it can be a disaster. When one wants to outshine the other, it will never work, no matter how much physical chemistry they have together. The relationship will quickly fizzle, as it did for Katy Perry and Russell Brand.

This photo on the following page says it all. It seems to me that Russell Brand may have had a hard time adjusting to his wife's fame and stardom. After looking at countless photos of the two of them as their marriage was unraveling, it seemed to me that Russell was miserable, which in turn made Katy sad and miserable. She even cried about their faltering relationship in her documentary film. It seemed to me that Russell may have wanted to be the one who was a bigger star. In this photo, note how he blocks Katy by getting in front of her, as she appears to be more in the background. This rude and hurtful behavior may have been reflective of the dynamic in their relationship.

In addition, contrast the pleasant expression on Katy's face with Russell's intense stare. He seems to be more focused on the camera than he is on his wife. He is literally stepping into her space. This is not a good sign in terms of relationship dynamics. No relationship can ever work if one of the parties is jealous of or competitive with the other. Thus, it came as no surprise to me when the couple finally parted ways.

Photo 11-6: Russell Brand appears to be hogging the limelight from Katy Perry. Note, too, their mismatched facial expressions. Photo credit: Jen Lowery/Splash News.

CONTROLLING BEHAVIOR

When one of the parties in a relationship is constantly "handling" the other—guiding her into position, grabbing her hand, and pulling her along—it is not a good sign. I noticed these signs and many others whenever I was asked by the press to analyze the body language of Jennifer Lopez and her husband, Marc Anthony.

He always seemed to be positioning her or pulling her in back of him, and she never seemed happy about it. In fact, she often looked awkward and uncomfortable. It seemed to me that throughout the years they were together, she tried to make things work and go along with what he wanted, but her body language and the expressions on her face showed that she was unhappy.

The tension between the two may also have been a result of two stars colliding and all the pressures that brings into a relationship. When they split up, it came as no surprise to me. It also came as no surprise that "J-Lo" finally looked happy and less tense; one could even see the genuine smiles that were lacking during their marriage. When someone is constantly seen pulling or positioning the other person, it is not a good sign for the longevity of the relationship.

Photo 11-7: Marc Anthony "handling" Jennifer Lopez. Photo credit: Whittle/Splash News.

NOT RECIPROCATING AFFECTION

When one member of a couple shows more affection than the other, or when one person in a relationship exhibits a closed-off body language, it can presage impending doom. Based on his body language vis a vis wife, Elin, Tiger Woods obviously had some affection issues well before his cheating scandal erupted.

Photo 11-8: Tiger Woods not reciprocating Elin Nordegren's affectionate gesture. This was taken years before the scandal of his multiple affairs broke. Photo credit: Phil Penman/Splash News.

In the photo we see Elin leaning toward Tiger, with her arm around his back and her hand lovingly draped over his shoulder. But Tiger is looking straight ahead, with his arms resting on his knees and his hands cupped directly in front, with a stiff, rigid posture. He doesn't reach over to touch Elin, but instead appears to have one hand touching the cuff of his shirt. Perhaps his mind was too preoccupied with the many other women with whom he was allegedly involved to focus his attention and affections on Elin.

Nothing was more shocking than seeing the photo of what singer Rihanna's boyfriend, rapper Chris Brown, did to her face. He pummeled her by banging her head on a car window and punching her in the face. This abused woman took out a restraining order against Chris, and he suffered the consequences by having to make legal restitution for his egregious actions. But unfortunately, as so many abused women do, Rihannna returned to her abuser. She announced on Oprah that they were back together and wanted the world's blessing.

Photo 11-9: Singer Chris Brown not reciprocating Rihanna's affections. Photo Ccedit: London Entertainment/Splash News.

But after seeing countless photos of the two of them together since then, it seems to me that Rihanna may be headed for more of the same trouble. Maybe Chris won't beat her, but this photo shows that he may be emotionally abusive, in my view at least. Chris is absorbed in the basketball game, but he ignores Rihanna's affection. There is no hand-holding nor any acknowledgment that she is even there. This same dynamic can be seen in many other photos of the couple. When they appeared at the 2013 Grammy Awards, Rihanna tried to be affectionate and put her head on Chris's shoulder, but he did not appear to reciprocate. She was seen in most photos holding onto herself, as if in mute protest.

It appears that Rihanna is crying out for love and affection from Chris, but in this photo, at least, it looks as though her needs are not being met. In my view, that does not bode well for this couple's future if things continue like this. Affection has to be reciprocated if a relationship has any chance of lasting.

CHAPTER 12

A PROFILE OF THE MOST TOXIC LIAR OF ALL: THE PSYCHOPATH/SOCIOPATH

Perhaps the scariest of all liars are the ones who exhibit antisocial behaviors. They are the organized and methodical psychopaths (like cannibal Jeffrey Dahmer and serial killer Ted Bundy) and the more disorganized and impulsive sociopaths (like wife and unborn baby killer Scott Peterson). Despite these and other subtle differences, they tend to share essentially the same traits.

In this chapter you will discover the profile of the psychopath or sociopath. You will learn about some common body and facial language "tells" that may indicate you're in the presence of one of these conscienceless individuals. Understanding this profile and learning about these common "tells" may help save your life, as you learn how to recognize these toxic and dangerous people who comprise just one to two percent of the population. (Note: For expediency I will refer to them as just psychopaths, but keep in mind that the terms are not interchangeable.)

SPEECH PATTERNS

Psychopaths are most easily recognized by their distinctive speech patterns. Constant use of the past tense can be an indicator of psychological detachment. Indeed, researchers have found that psychopaths use the past tense more often than the present tense as compared to nonpsychopaths, especially when describing their crimes. They also tend to have a more disjointed speaking style, replete with filler words such as "uh" and "um" that interrupt the flow of speech. This is likely because this allows the psychopath more time to think about the lies he must concoct. It is their attempt to try and control their words.

Because psychopaths are entitled and see the world and others as theirs for the taking, researchers the University of British Columbia found that they used more words such as "because" and "so that"—basically, cause and effect statements. This indicates that they tend to view their crime as the logical outcome of a plan, something that "had" to be done to achieve a goal. They will also lie and use charm to take what they see as theirs. Thus, a psychopath may try to cajole you by excessively complimenting or flattering you. For this reason, such people usually make a good first impressions because they are highly attuned to peoples' reactions and then saying what they want to hear. They will also ask a lot of questions to quickly figure out your emotional hot buttons—what makes you sad, angry, or happy—so they can play upon those emotions (emotions they lack, by the way). They have no feelings; no remorse, and certainly no conscience. Their verbal manipulations can be persistent and inexorable.

As charming and engaging as they try to be, they will often inadvertently reveal who they are through an insensitive, unfeeling remark or comment; you may even hear a disturbing sadistic or macabre comment. Never ignore your body's response to something like this, as it is warning you that something is very wrong with the person in front of you. As well, most psychopaths have had a history of being cruel to animals, so don't be surprised if you hear an insensitive or sadistic comment about your pet.

Studies also show that psychopaths seem to be most occupied with basic needs, such as food, shelter, clothing, and the like. They tend to use twice as many words related to these basic physiological needs and self-preservation as nonpsychopaths. In contrast, nonpsychopathic murderers will talk more about spirituality, religion, and family.

If a psychopath commits a crime, he or she (usually he) will often speak of himself as the victim, just as Aileen Wuornos did, a serial killer who blamed her actions on the police (for allowing her to keep killing numerous men) as well as society (for allowing her to be sentenced to death). As she maintained in her final interview the night before she was executed, "I didn't do anything as wrong as they said...and I saved a lot of people's butts from getting hurt, and raped, and killed." Charles Manson does a lot of this kind of blameshifting from behind bars, as well. Like most psychopaths she also expressed a grandiose opinion of herself. This type of grandiose speaking has also been evident in the many interviews Charles Manson has granted throughout the years. This over-inflated sense of self is due to the psychopath's sense of entitlement, which yields a certain braggadocio and cockiness. Thus, the psychopath will speak of himself in grandiose terms while blaming others and taking absolutely no responsibility for his actions.

Psychopaths are, surprisingly, highly sensitive to what they perceive as slights against them. They can respond in kind by becoming verbally or even physically hostile. Perhaps the most chilling thing I've ever seen is a video of psychopathic murderer Richard Kuklinski being interviewed by psychiatrist Park Dietz. Kuklinski informs Dietz that the psychiatrist made him angry but doesn't know why. When the doctor asks him if he felt that he was being judged and whether that was what angered him, the serial killer openly admits that to be the case.

Psychopaths who don't kill also tend to go on the defensive if they feel they are being judged or criticized. They will verbally assault you with a barrage of hostile words. They also tend to hyperarticulate or precisely pronounce their words when they are lying. You can see this clearly in serial killer Ted Bundy's last prison interview, hours before he was to be executed. When the garden-variety sociopath uses this precise, staccato articulation and stops using contractions, know that he is most probably lying. This clipped speaking pattern could also be heard in the courtroom when financial swindler Bernard Madoff made his final "apology" before he was taken away to spend the rest of his life behind bars. The staccato tone may have also been a reflection of hostile or mocking feelings toward his victims.

Perhaps the most telling speech pattern of the psychopath is that they will often contradict themselves, even within a single sentence. For example, they will lie or omit information when you ask them a question, but they may tell you the truth if you rephrase the question slightly. Researchers have discovered that this has to do with the particular way their brain is wired.

VOCAL TONES

Because psychopaths show no remorse and indeed harbor no feelings of guilt, their vocal tone mirrors this lack of feeling and emotion. In analyzing the voice patterns of such notorious serial killers as Jeffrey Dahmer, John Wayne Gacey, Ted Bundy, "Nightstalker" Richard Ramirez, and Mafia hit man Richard Kuklinski, there is one overriding distinct similarity: they all speak or spoke in a monotone devoid of emotion, seemingly detached as they spoke of their heinous crimes. Even in those sociopaths who are not murderers, you can hear a dead, hollow monotone. This was evident in Ponzi schemer Bernard Madoff's voice, for example. This monotone is particularly evident when the sociopath is blaming others and saying that it is everyone else's fault but his own. You will sometimes hear them deviate from their normally monotone speech when they are trying to manipulate someone. They will get louder, the pace of their speech will quicken, and the pitch of their voice may go up as they try to enroll people in their schemes.

CROCODILE TEARS

If you ever see a psychopath shed a tear, as many do during court proceedings, you will notice that they are empty or fake tears. First, there are usually no actual tears involved. Second, they will often be seen wiping underneath each eye, one at a time. When people cry genuine tears they cry with both eyes, and so they will tend to wipe both eyes at once. As well, the small muscles on either side of their bottom lip droops downward. When the psychopath cries, you won't see any of this. Instead, you'll see that the lower lip will remain stationary or even turn upward in a slender smile called "duping delight." In essence, the psychopath's delight in his ability to fool others leaks out in his facial expressions and movements. In Diane Sawyer's interview with Scott Peterson, this was the dead giveaway that he was lying and faking his distress over not knowing where his pregnant wife was, when of course he knew all along where she was—at the bottom of the bay. The same held true for Susan Smith, who will be spending the rest of her life behind bars for killing her children. When she gave a press conference and cried about her missing children, her fake tears were actually what raised suspicions that she was the killer.

When people cry genuine tears they usually don't go immediately from tears to a neutral or happy state. There is a lag or transitional time required before the different emotional state can set in. With the psychopath there is no transition time needed, as they can switch from tears to smiles in a millisecond—another indication of deception. As Scott Peterson and Susan Smith and countless others have done, psychopaths will often feign emotion by crying in order to gain sympathy and suck people in.

FACIAL EXPRESSION

Because the psychopath lies and manipulates so well, it is important to pay close attention to his gaze. If he stares at you without looking away, know that he is likely out to manipulate. This weighty stare is a type of control. This was quite evident in former Illinois police officer Drew Peterson, who now sits in prison for killing one of his four wives. If you watch his *Today Show* interview years before he was convicted, you will see this intense, compelling gaze as he attempts to convince the host and the public of his innocence. When a psychopath has little to gain from you, however, he will have a hard time maintaining eye contact because he cannot relate to other people as separate entities. They only see people as objects, vehicles to satisfy their desires and needs.

The psychopath will also endeavor to manipulate by playing a kind of cat-and-mouse game: intensely staring at you and then suddenly completely ignoring you. This is essentially intermittent operant conditioning; it's meant to keep you off balance and vulnerable (and hence more likely to be bullied and manipulated).

The smile of a psychopath is almost never genuine. They don't smile naturally, with the apples of their cheeks raised and their eyes squinting and teeth showing. Instead it's a mask-like, tight-lipped smile that looks phony, as though they are mimicking a smile. Because they are essentially devoid of emotions, many psychopaths have trained themselves to maintain a pleasant expression on their face so that others won't see the coldness in their soul. Ironically, they end up alienating many people this way because they lack a normal range of emotion through their facial expressions. That may be the reason why serial killer John Wayne Gacy dressed up as a clown and painted a happy expression on his emotionless face, in his efforts to lure young boys.

BODY LANGUAGE

Psychopaths will usually display their emotional reactions—usually rage—via the their autonomic nervous system. You may see them suddenly sweat or their skin flush as they literally heat up with anger. While they may keep a cool, calm, and collected tone, their skin belies them. They will also often move in closer or lean in toward others when they speak. They will also often sit with their hands interlocked, with a rigid, fixed body posture. When Drew Peterson appeared on the *Today Show* to discuss his missing wife Stacy Peterson, he sat there with hands clasped and did not deviate from his body position throughout the entire interview. The psychopath is not able to feel or express the full range of emotions (other than rage), so their body movements tend to be similarly mechanical and artificial. It is also not common to see them holding on to themselves as they remain in that immobile position.

The psychopath will often contradict what he says with his body language. For example, while saying yes, he will shake his head to mean no, and vice versa. While his words say one thing, his body language tell a different story.

It is also not uncommon to see a puffed-out chest and a swagger in his walk. Even though Drew Peterson was in shackles, wearing his orange jailhouse jumpsuit, he still managed to present a cocky demeanor as he proceeded to his trial. Even with this air of cockiness and self-confidence, the psychopath may still inadvertently show that he had something to hide, as you could see in the previous photo of convicted child molester and former Penn State football coach Jerry Sandusky on his way to the courtroom for his trial. While he is all smiles, the fact that he is walking with his hands in both of his pockets shows that he had something to hide—his guilt.

Since the psychopath's aim is to lure you in, he will often feign illness or a physical ailment to incur sympathy. This is precisely what Ted Bundy did. He used a removable cast on his arm to feign injury and lure in hapless young women.

CONCLUSION
THE CATHARSIS OF DISCOVERY

There is often a great deal of satisfaction that comes from discovering that someone is or has been lying to you. There is even more satisfaction when you learn that they were held accountable for their actions. For instance, Marsha Petrie Sue, the woman who copied from one of my books and ended up losing the Federal court case I filed against her, is now and forever known as a copyright infringer. Because of her actions, she also lost her certification by the National Speakers Association for a time.

It is cathartic to hear about people like Tawana Brawley, who falsely accused 10 innocent men of attacking and raping her, and who must now pay restitution to the prosecutor whom she falsely accused. It is also rewarding to know that Amani Ginyard, who falsely accused her husband of molesting their daughters, must now pay thousands of dollars in restitution while also losing custody of her daughters. You may seek solace in the fact that "karmic justice" sometimes prevails, as it did in the case of O.J. Simpson, who finally ended up in prison, not for killing his wife, Nicole, and her friend, Ron Goldman, but for another, unrelated crime. Drew Peterson ended up in jail for the murder of his third wife, after suspicions were raised when his fourth wife went missing.

It's also satisfying to see karmic justice at work in your personal life. Perhaps the woman whose lies cost you your job, is now jobless and hasn't been able to find work for years, while you have flourished. It may make you smile to learn that your ex-husband, who cheated on you with his secretary, is now sad and alone because she left him for another man. It feels even better knowing that he is miserable and his life is a mess, while you have once again found true love and feel that life is just beginning.

It is also a huge relief to see criminal justice served, where the likes of Bernard Madoff, Scott Peterson, Jerry Sandusky, and other murderers, rapists, and con men and women will never be able to destroy anyone else's life ever again. They will never again experience freedom as they and many others like them will remain behind bars until their dying day.

The verdict is still out in terms of what will happen to cyclist Lance Armstrong. Will he receive real justice or karmic justice? Regardless, all of this shows us that the old saying "cheaters and liars never prosper" is true. One way or another, all the toxic lying—the deception, the cheating, the dissembling, the phoniness—eventually catches up with the liar.

Perhaps you have been lied to and duped and you had no idea it was coming. Other times, maybe you saw it coming and are now kicking yourself for not listening to your instincts. By reading this book you have learned that you never need to feel helpless again. You have learned to recognize the signs—the "tells"—that show you someone is not being honest. You have seen firsthand, through the words on these pages and through the photographs of those who have deceived, that the body doesn't lie. Neither does the face, the voice, or the choice of words. After reading the actual words liars have spoken, you have discovered that what people say and how they say it can no longer be overlooked.

You have learned that if you look at body and facial language and pay attention to voice and speech patterns, you can gain a full and clear picture of whether or not someone is telling you the truth. Now you know that you must objectively see and hear what *is*, and not what you want it to be. Use this book as a reference. Don't hesitate to return to it from time to time and reread salient passages—or the whole thing! The more you put into practice what you learn from the pages in this book, more proficient you will be at weeding out the liars and cheats who are already in your life or who want to enter your life. You will now know with confidence whether your husband, wife, lover, friend, sibling, son or daughter, parents, or other relative is lying. You will now know if your friends really are true friends, or whether your business associates are being forthright. You will now be able to tell if salespeople, politicians, and even newsmakers who appear regularly in the media are telling it like is or simply blowing smoke.

Now you have all the tools that will allow you to determine whether someone is friend or foe. So go out in the world and use them judiciously, and never be victimized by anyone's lies ever again!

INDEX

achievements, embellishing your, 52

actions, context of, 75-76

Adam's apple,
  autonomic nervous system
    and the, 99
  covering the, 104

adolescence, monitoring, 43

affection, unreciprocated, 192-195

age, lying about your, 50-51, 57

anger,
  high-pitched voice and, 156
  righteous indignation and,
    152-153
  tone of voice and, 160

animals, 33-38

Aniston, Jennifer, nose scratching,
  137-138

answers, evasive, 174-175

Anthony,
  Casey, 53
  Cindy, 53

Anthony, Marc, controlling
  behavior of, 191-192

anxiety,
  nervous laughter and, 167
  ways to relieve, 107-108

Arias, Jodi, 89
  voice, tone of, 164

arm crossing, 104-105

arms and hands, changes in the,
  100-117

arms, hiding the, 113-115

Armstrong, Lance, 29, 51
  baseline of, 76

blameshifting of, 171-172
body language of, 100
breathing patterns of, 78
clenched jaw of, 152
cupping hands of, 116-117
excuses of, 179-180
eye contact of, 123
facial sweating of, 82-83
fake smile of, 141
glaring of, 129
hard swallowing and, 100
head movements of, 92
head position of, 95
look of surprise and, 131-132
mouth movements of, 101-102
palm position of, 110-111
pursed lips of, 148
second person phrasing of, 180
skin changes of, 81
speaking tone of, 159
squinting and, 135
attacking
comments, 60
tones of voice, 161-162
authority figures, boundaries and, 43
autonomic nervous system, 81, 90, 98
Adam's apple and the, 99
salivary gland and the, 139
the nose and the, 137
avoidance of eye contact, deception and, 122-123
backing up, the motion of, 87-88
baseline, establishing a, 75-76, 121-122
behavior, controlling, 191-192

betrayal, 25-27
biting, finger and nail, 100
blameshifting, 171-172
blinking, rapid eye, 132-133
blood flow, evidence of increased, 81
body parts, covering vulnerable, 103-104
body, physical changes in your, 74
Bonds, Barry, 85
shoulder position of, 86
boundaries, authority figures and, 43
Brand, Russell, physical chemistry of, 190
Brawley, Tawana, 29-30
breathing changes, 77-79
breathing patterns, deception and, 78
Brown, Chris,
affection toward Rihanna and, 193-195
head movements of, 94
posture of, 83
Bundy, Ted, 197
fake injury of, 203
verbal assault of, 199
Bush, George W., speech patterns of, 170-171
business deals, being weary of, 58
business, betrayal in, 27
cadence and pacing, speaking, 164-167
Carey, Mariah, 91
shoulder movements of, 106

Index

Carr, Judy Feld, 54

catatonic
numbness, betrayal and, 25
stance, 90

Catfish, 67

catfishing, 63-64, 66-70
Manti Te'o and, 69-70

celebrity liars, 24-25

children,
eye rubbing and, 133
pigeon-toed stance of, 119

chimpanzees, facial expressions of, 34-35

choppy cadence, 165-166

clenched jaw, 151-152

Clinton, Bill, 52
finger pointing of, 112-113
glaring of, 130
lip biting of, 148
perspiration changes in, 82
pursed lips of, 147
righteous indignation of, 153-154

cold shoulder, the, 104-105

collar tugging, 98-99

comments, self-deprecating, 62

compliments, 173-174

conditioning,
negative emotional, 42
negative physical, 42

consistency of statements, 60

contentiousness, 175-176

context and instincts, 73-76

contractions, avoiding, 174

controlling behavior, 191-192

conversation, reciprocal, 63

cotton mouth, 139-140

creaky tone of voice, 159

crimes of passion, 25-27

Crist Jr., Harry, 30

Cruise, Tom, foot position of, 118, 188-189

curt responses, 61-62

cyber liars, 57-70

cyber scammers, 60

Dahmer, Jeffrey, 197

dating, online, 57

deception,
avoidance of eye contact and, 122-123
breathing patterns and, 78
infants and, 38
lip biting and, 145

deceptive behavior,
dolphins and, 35
elephants and, 34-35

defensiveness, 175-176
staring and, 128

deflecting, 171-172

deliberate and slow speech, 166-167

depression, betrayal and, 25

detaching, 180

details, professing too many, 61

development, lying as part of our, 32

Dietz, Park, 199-200

disbelief, squinting and, 134

dolphins, deceptive behavior and, 35

dropped jaw, 150-151

dry throat, 99

Edwards, John, 28-29, 53
    eye blinking of, 133
    eye contact of, 125
    fake smile of, 142
    forward leaning of, 90
    hand gestures of, 103
    lip swing of, 146
    posture of, 85
    skin changes in, 80

egocentrism, 63

elephants, deceptive behavior and, 34-35

emotional conditioning, 42

emotions, the limbic system and, 155-156

evasive answers, 174-175

excuses, making, 179-180

experiences, embellishing, 51

expression, incongruent facial, 177

expressions, facial, 75

eye contact,
    avoiding, 122-123, 125
    breaking, 122
    lack of, 74

eye movement, thoughts and, 122

eye rubbing, 133

eyebrows, raised, 136

eyes of surprise, 130-132

eyes,
    covering the, 125
    shifty, 133-134

facial expression, incongruent, 177

facial
    expressions, 75
    expressions of psychopaths, 201-202
    language, 121-154
    sweat, 81-82

fading out while speaking, 158-159

failures, discussing, 52

fake online profiles, 61

fake smile, 140-144

fast speech, 164-165

fast-talking people, 164

fear, rapid eye blinking and, 132

feelings,
    building up a person's, 48
    lying to avoid hurt, 47-48

feet, position of the, 117-119

fidgeting, 90-91

fight-or-flight response, 90

filler words, 172

finances,
    lying about your, 57
    overly focused on, 62

finger biting, 100

finger-pointing, 112-113
    angry, 82

Index

flared nostrils, 138

flattery, 173-174

flirtation, 48

flushed, skin becoming, 80

foot position, 188-190
importance of, 115

forehead, wrinkled, 136

frenetic speech, 164-165

Freudian slips, 180-181

Frey, Amber, 89, 159

Ginyard, Darryl, 30-31

glaring, 129-130

grade-school liars, 41-42

grammar, poor, 63

greed, 32

grooming, hand, 107-110

guilt trips, 65

gulping, 99-100

habitual liars, the creation of, 41-42

hand
grooming, 107-110
picking, 107-110
rubbing, 107-110
tapping, 107-110
wringing, 107-110

hands and arms, changes in the, 100-117

hands,
cupping, 116-117
hiding the, 113-115

handshake, clammy, 74

Harris, Clara, 26

Harris, David, 26

head
bow, 93-94
cock, 94-96
jerk, 92-93
position, changes in, 91-100
tilt, 94-96

Heene, Falcon, 101-102

Heene, Mayumi, hand gestures of, 109-110

Heene, Richard,
attacking tone of, 161-162
frenetic tone of voice, 165
jaw position of, 150
nose scratching of, 137
righteous indignation of, 152-153, 176
use of filler words by, 172-173

height, lying about your, 57

high pitch, 156

Holmes, Katie, foot position of, 118, 188-189

honesty,
facial language and, 122
phrases of speech for, 172-173

hostile comments, 60

hostility, the meaning of, 113

Humphries, Kris, 187-188

Hunter, Rielle, 29, 53, 90, 142

hurting others' feelings, 47-48

image, presenting a favorable, 50-52

inappropriate smile, 146-147

incongruent facial expression, 177

inconsistences in truth-telling, 175

infant liars, 36-38

information, giving up too much, 169-171

instincts and context, 73-76

intimacy, eye contact and problems with, 123

itching and scratching, 106-107

jaw movements and positioning, 149-152

jealousy, 32

job, lying about your, 57

Jolie, Angelina, hand position of, 114-115

Jones, Star, 24

Judeo-Christian beliefs, 20-21

jutting jaw, 149

Kardashian, Kim, 187-188

Kuklinski, Richard, 199-200

Kutcher, Ashton, 184-185

laughter, nervous, 167

leaning forward, 88-90

licking, lip, 139-140

limbic system,
    emotions and the, 155-156
    eye movement and the, 122
    lying symbols and the, 100

lip
    biting, 144-145, 148

licking, 139-140
    swing, 144-146

lips, pursed, 147

little white lie, definition of a, 24

Lohan, Dina, 25

Lohan, Lindsay, 25
    eye movement of, 131
    hand movements of, 108-109
    jaw position of, 150
    palm position of, 110-111
    whiny tone of, 162

Lopez, Jennifer, Marc Anthony's controlling behavior toward, 191-192

love, online, 58-59

low pitch, 156-157

Madoff, Bernard, 26
    eye contact of, 124-125
    facial expression of, 177
    fake smile of, 143
    flattery of, 173
    speaking volume of, 157, 159
    staring trait of, 126-128

malice, 32

Manson, Charles, blameshifting of, 199

Minaj, Nicki, 91
    eye movement of, 134
    shoulder movements of, 105

monotone voice, 163

Moore, Demi, 184-185

motivating others, 54-55

mouth,
    changes in the, 139-148

cotton, 139-140
covering the, 101-102

movements, slow, 74

nail biting, 100

names, odd, 63-64

narcissism, 63

nastiness, 60-61

neck touching, 96-98

neck tugging, 98-99

needy personalities, 59

negative emotional conditioning, 42

negative physical conditioning, 42

nervous laughter, 167

nervousness, tone of voice and, 160

New Testament, references to lying in the, 19

Ninth Commandment, meaning of the, 19

Nixon, Richard, eye movement of, 133

nonsensical speech, 181

nose, movements and gestures of the, 137-138

nostrils, flared, 138

obsequiousness, 173-174

odd names, 63-64

Old Testament references to lying in the, 19

online dating, 57

online, lying, 57

overly long pauses, 178

pacing and cadence, speaking, 164-167

pacing of speech, 155-167

Pacino, Al, neck touching pose of, 97-97

Pagones, Steven, 30

palm positions, 110-111

pathological liars, the creation of, 41-42

Pattinson, Robert, 24-25

pauses, overly long, 178

Perry, Katy, physical chemistry of, 190

Perry, Richard, 66-67

perspiration,
presence of, 80
upper lip, 82

Peterson, Drew, 89
body language of, 202
eye contact of, 128
head position of, 95
rigidity of, 90
speaking tone of, 160
throat clearing and, 161

Peterson, Scott,
head movements of, 92
posture of, 89
speaking tone of, 159

photos that lie, 65-66

physical changes in your body, 74

picking, hand, 107-110

pigeon-toed stance, 117
children and the, 119

pitch, 155-167
    high, 156
    low, 156-157
Pitt, Brad, hand position of, 114-115
pointing, finger, 112-113
posture changes, 83-91
preschool liars, 40
protecting others, 53-54
psychological detachment, psychopaths and, 198
psychopaths, 197-203
    tone of voice and, 163
punishment as children, the creation of liars and the, 42
punishment, avoiding, 52-53
pursed lips, 147
question, repeating a, 174-175
questions,
    asking too many, 61-62
    statements that sound like, 178
rage, betrayal and, 25
rapid eye blinking, 132-133
raspy tone of voice, 159
reassurance, phrases of speech for, 172-173
reciprocal conversation, 63
Reddy, Vasudevi, 38
rejection, avoiding, 50-52
relationships, body language in, 183-195
religious doctrines, lying and, 19

repeating a question, 174-175
Ressam, Ahmed, facial sweating of, 83
righteous indignation, 152-153, 176-177
rigid stance, 90
Rihanna, 83, 94
    affection toward Chris Brown and, 193-195
Rimes, LeAnn, 25
rubbing, eye, 133
rubbing, hand, 107-110
saliva production, lying and, 99
salivary glands, autonomic nervous system and the, 139
Sandusky, Jerry,
    awkward silence of, 178
    fake smile of, 144
    posture of, 86
sarcasm, 60-61
scammers, cyber, 60
Schulman, Nev, 64, 67-68
Schwarzenegger, Arnold, 186
    fake smile of, 146-147
scratching and itching, 106-107
scratching, neck, 98-99
second person, referring to self in, 180
self-
    confidence, loss of, 85-86
    deprecating comments, 62
    preservation, lying for, 48-50
    righteous indignation, 135

Index

Seventh Commandment, meaning of the, 19

sex, conversations about, 64-65

sexual terminology, 64

shaky tone of voice, 160

shifty eyes, 133-134

shoulders, rounded, 84

shrugging, 86-87

Sickles, Daniel, 26

signal, throat-touching, 97

Simpson, O.J., 52
 breathing patterns of, 79
 collar tugging, 98
 cotton mouth and, 140
 finger pointing of, 113
 head movements of, 92
 head position of, 96
 jaw position of, 149, 151
 look of surprise and, 132
 posture of, 86-87
 raised eyebrows of, 136
 righteous indignation of, 153
 scratching movements of, 107
 second person phrasing of, 180
 speaking volume of, 158
 speech patterns of, 170
 squinting and, 135

skin changes, 80

slow and deliberate speech, 166-167

slow movements, 74

smile,
 fake, 140-144
 inappropriate, 146-147

smiles, fake, 80-81

Smith, Susan, lip swing of, 146

sneezing, 138

sob stories, being wary of, 59

social networking, 51

sociopaths, 197-203
 tone of voice and, 163

speaking too loudly, 158

speaking too softly, 157

speech content, 169-181

speech patterns of psychopaths, 198

speech,
 fast, 164-165
 frenetic, 164-165

spelling, poor, 63

squinting, 134-135

staccato cadence, 165-166

stammering, 166

stance, pigeon-toed, 117

staring, 126-128

statements that sound like questions, 178

statements,
 consistency of, 60
 context of, 75-76

status, lying about your, 57

Stewart, Kristen, 24-25

stiff posture, 83

stress, rapid eye blinking and, 132

stuttering, 166

surprise, eyes of, 130-132

survival, lying for, 49-50

suspicion, squinting and, 134

sweat, facial, 81-82

sweating, 81-82

sweet tone of voice, 163-164

talking too much, 169-171

Talmud, references to lying in the, 20

tangents, going off on, 169-171

tapping, hand, 107-110

Te'o, Manti, 51-52
    catfishing and, 69
    eye contact of, 123
    posture change in, 83-84

teenage liars, 42-43

Ten Commandments, lying and
    the, 19

terminology, sexual, 64

terrorists, fake smiles of, 147

third person, referring to self in, 180

throat clearing, constant, 161

throat, covering the, 96-98

toddler liars, 38-39

tone of voice,
    creaky, 159
    raspy, 159
    shaky, 160
    sweet, 163-164
    whiny, 162

tone, 155-167

tones, attacking of voice, 161-162

torso shielding, 104-105

truthfulness, concept of, 41

tugging, neck, 98-99

Twain, Mark, 46

ulterior motives, lying for, 48

upper lip perspiration, 82

verb tenses, incorrect, 174

verbal cues, 169

vocal tones of psychopaths, 200

volume, 155-167

vulnerability, arm crossing and, 104

vulnerable body parts, covering,
    103-104

walking in front of someone, 184-185

weight, lying about your, 57

whiny tone of voice, 162

Woods, Tiger,
    affection toward Elin
        Nordegren and, 193
    eye contact of, 125
    hand gestures of, 103-104
    head movements of, 93-94
    monotone voice of, 163
    pursed lips of, 147

words and body language, 100

words, filler, 172

wringing, hand, 107-110

wrinkled forehead, 136

Wuornos, Aileen, blameshifting of,
    171-172, 199

Young, Andrew Aldridge, 53

ABOUT THE AUTHOR

Dr. Lillian Glass is a well-respected behavioral analyst, body language expert, and communication expert. She regularly appears throughout the media on all major networks, in newspapers and magazines, and throughout the Web. She has appeared on such shows as *Entertainment Tonight, 20/20, Good Morning America, Dr. Phil, In Session, Today Show, Dancing With the Stars, Millionaire Matchmaker, HLN, CNN, Fox News, MSNBC, CNBC, Chelsea Lately,* and *The Daily Show with John Stewart.*

Dr. Glass has lectured on body language and deception to various law enforcement agencies, including the FBI. She also provides her expertise in the legal field as a legal consultant, jury consultant, and expert witness in the area of behavioral analysis and vocal forensics. Dr. Glass is also an experienced Mediator who received her training at The Straus Institute for Dispute Resolution at the Pepperdine University School of Law. She is the author of more than a dozen books, including the perennial best-seller, *Toxic People.*

Dr. Glass offers her services via her Website *www.lillianglass.com*, where the public is invited to submit photos and videos for her analysis, just she does with newsmakers in the media. You can learn more about Dr. Glass and her products at *www.drlillianglass.com*.